II am grateful to God for everything! And I believe that the meaning of life is to give meaning to other lives. L.E.I.LH, you are the meaning of my life.
Lov U

Luciana Gomes

2024

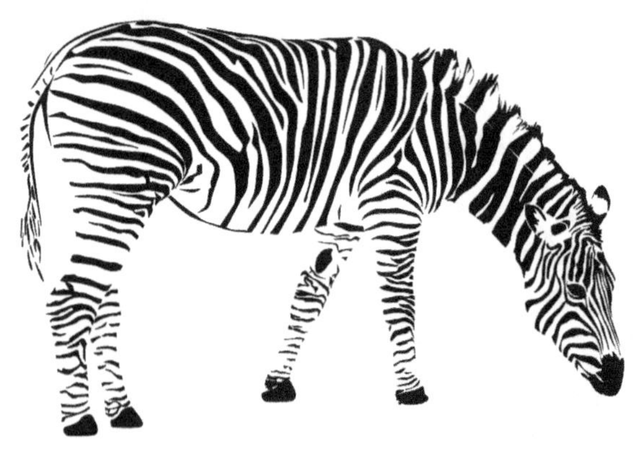

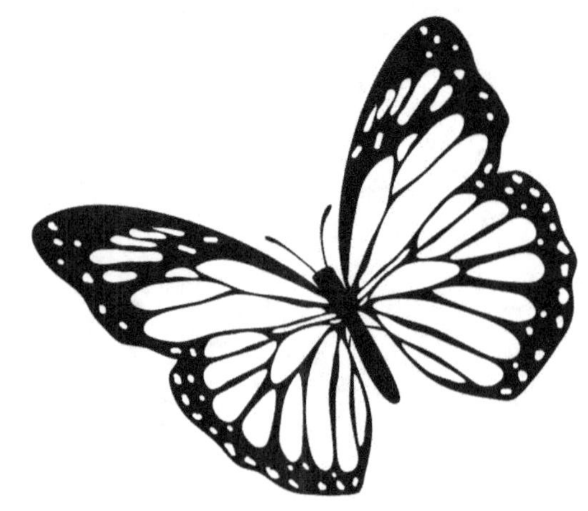

This Book Belongs to:

____

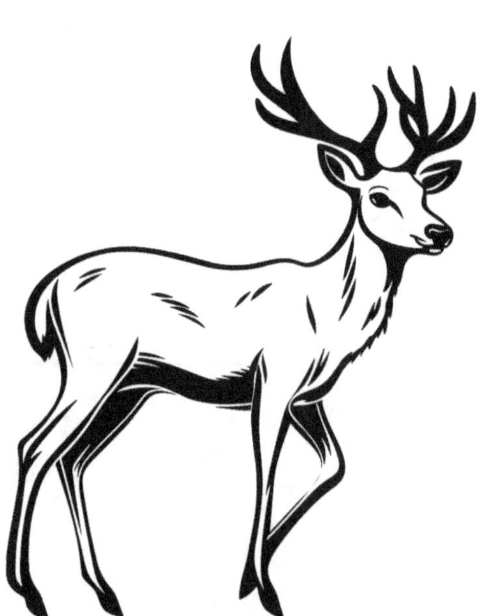

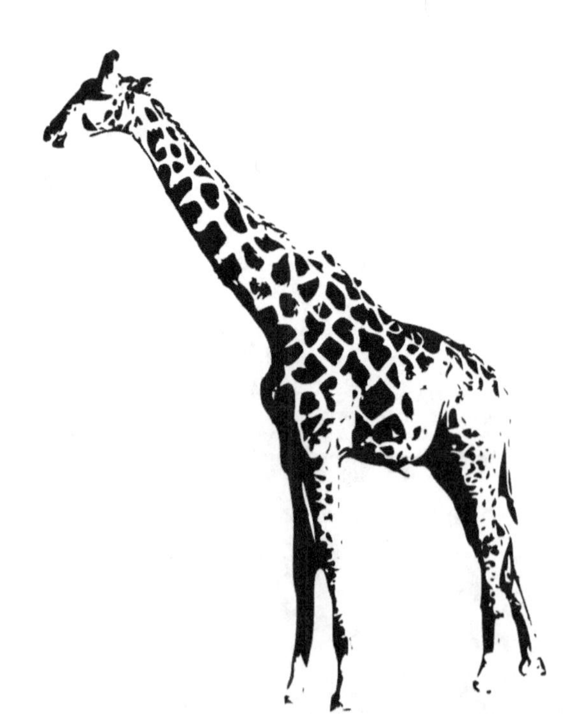

Test Color Page

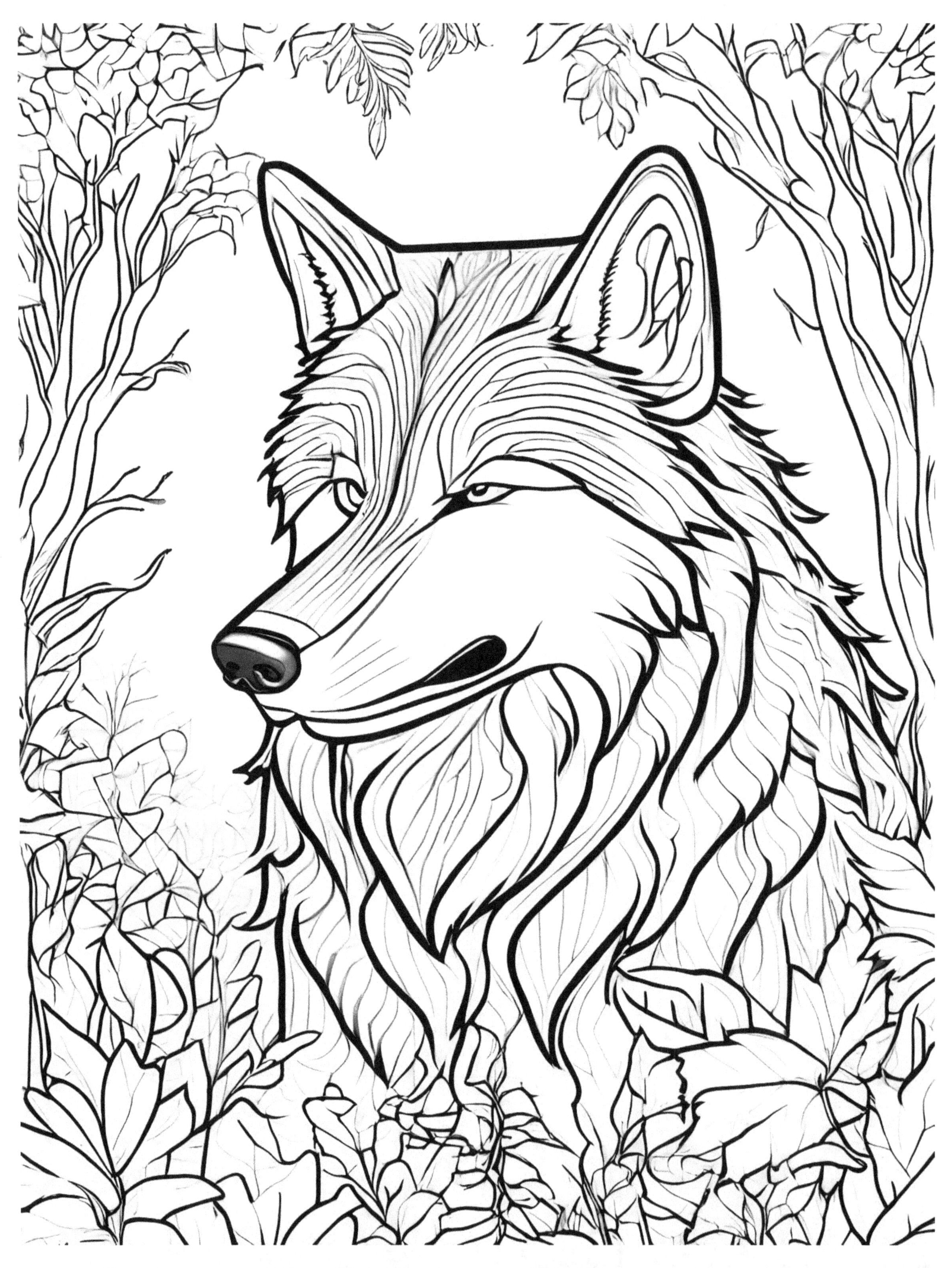

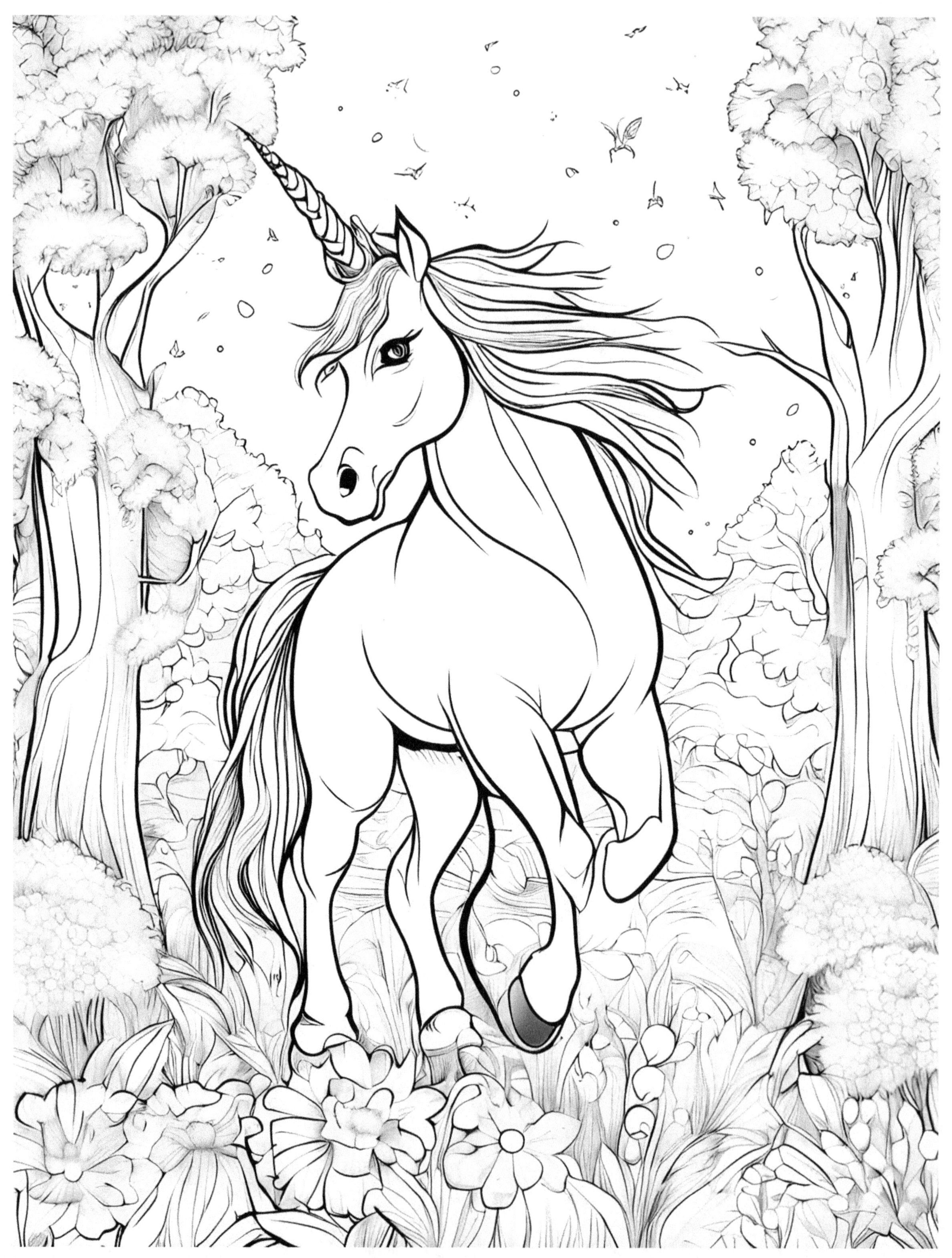

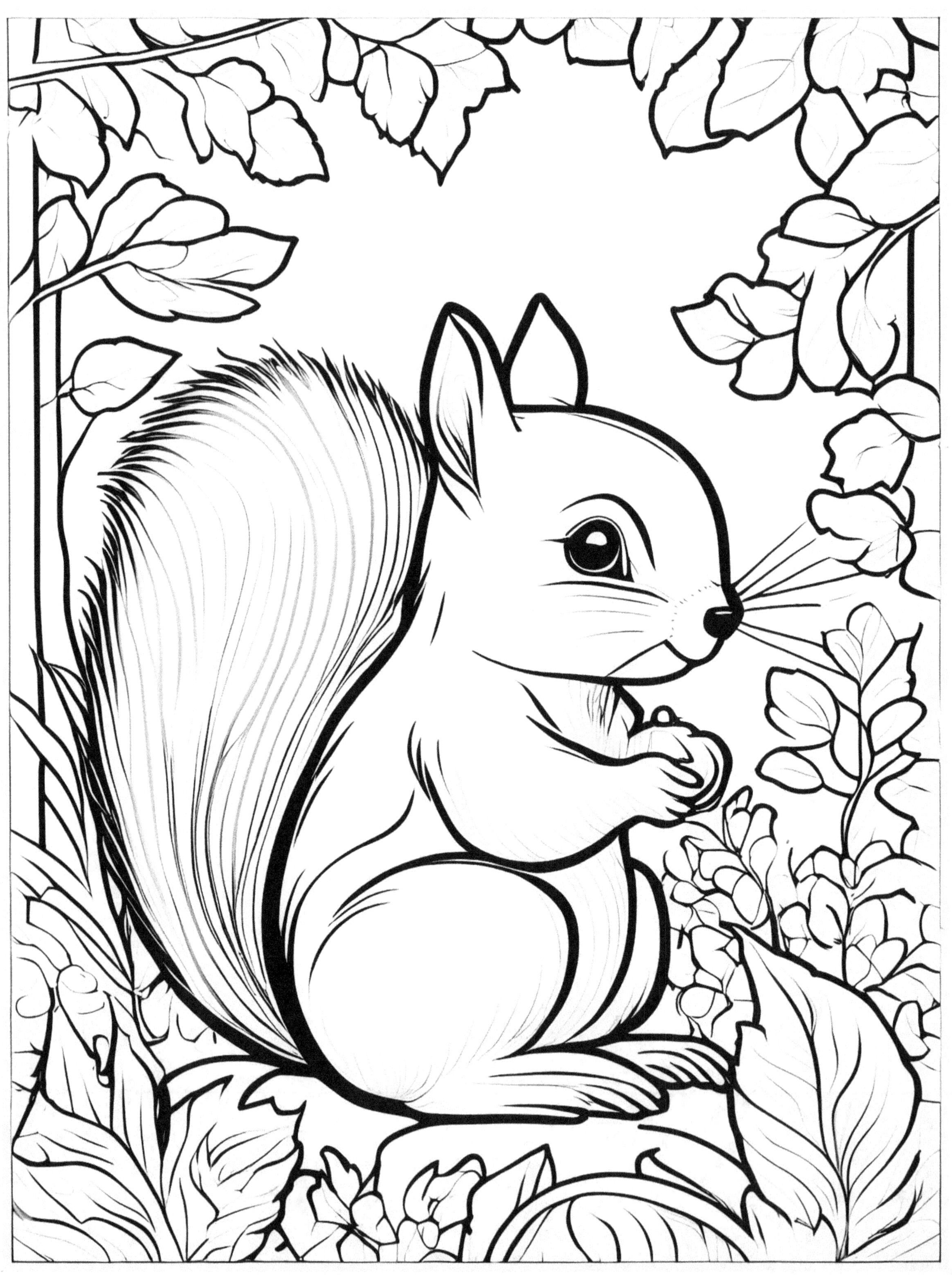

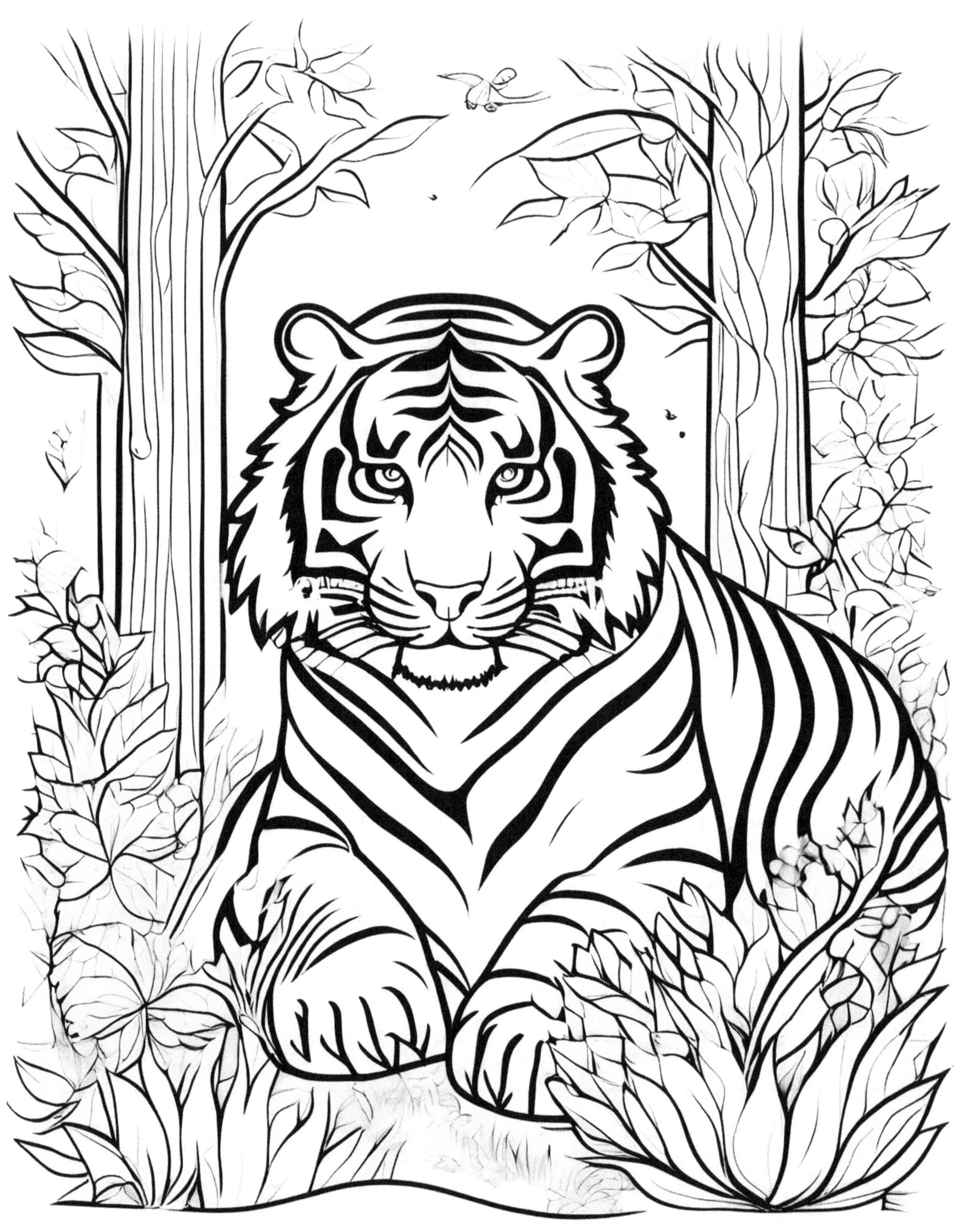

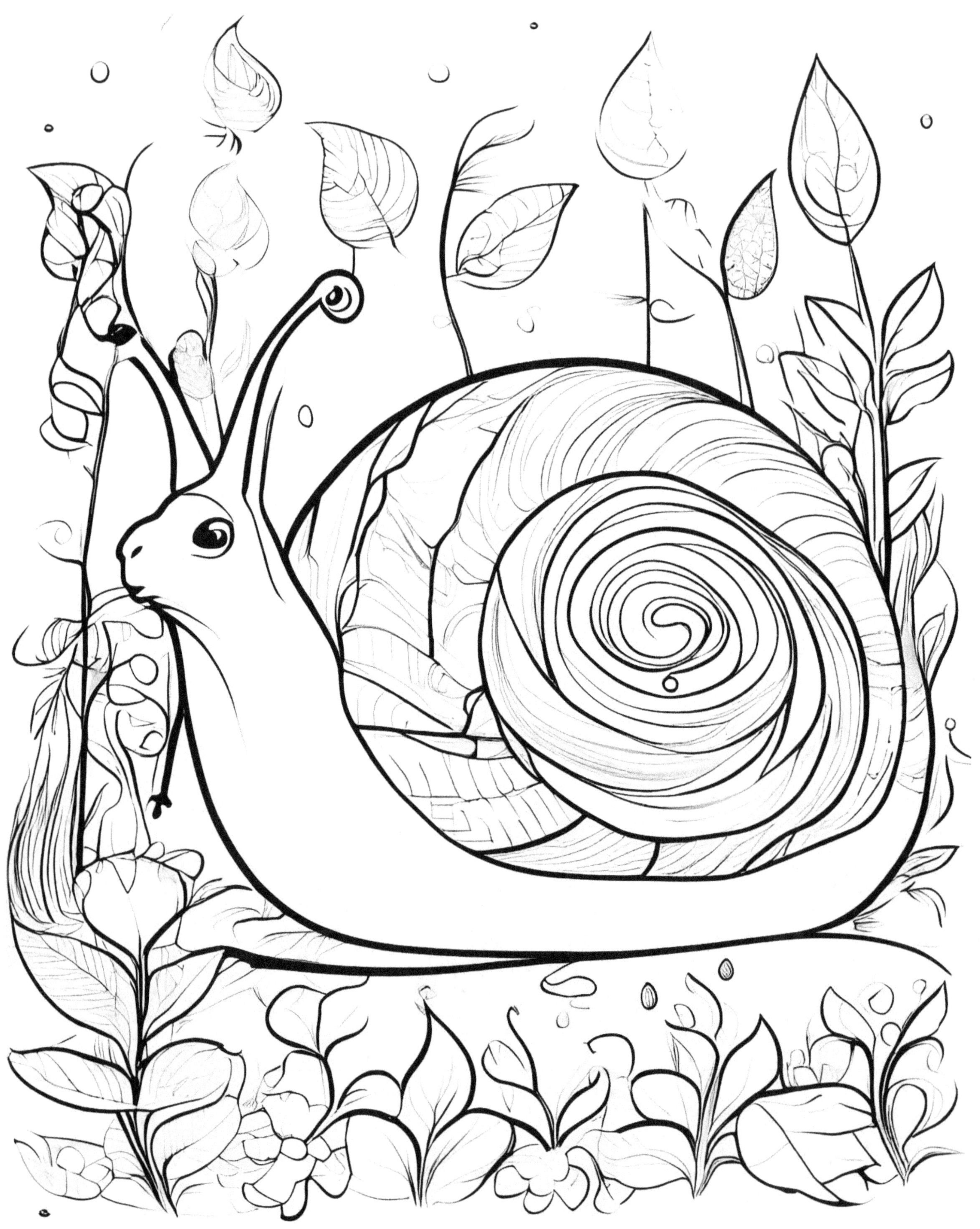

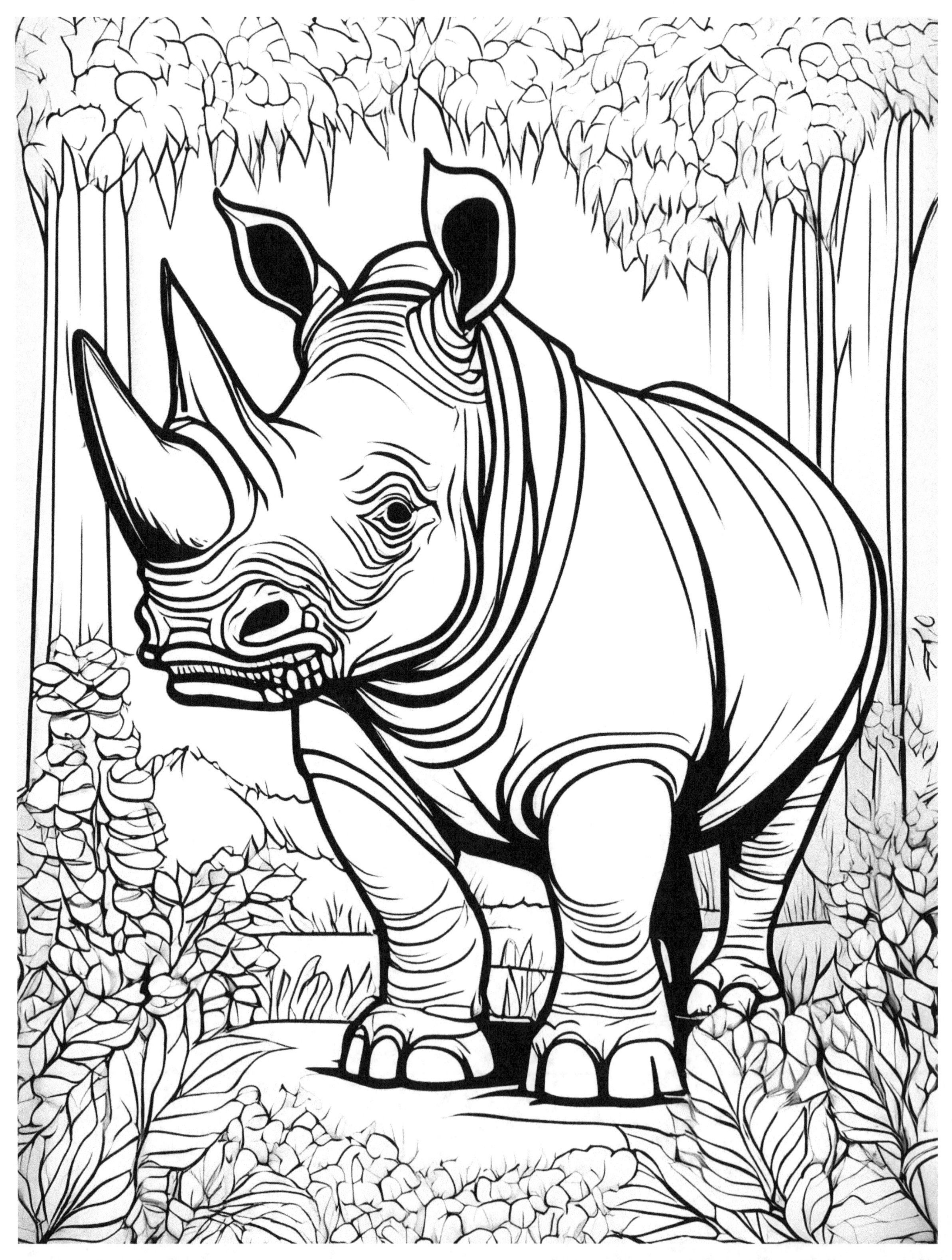

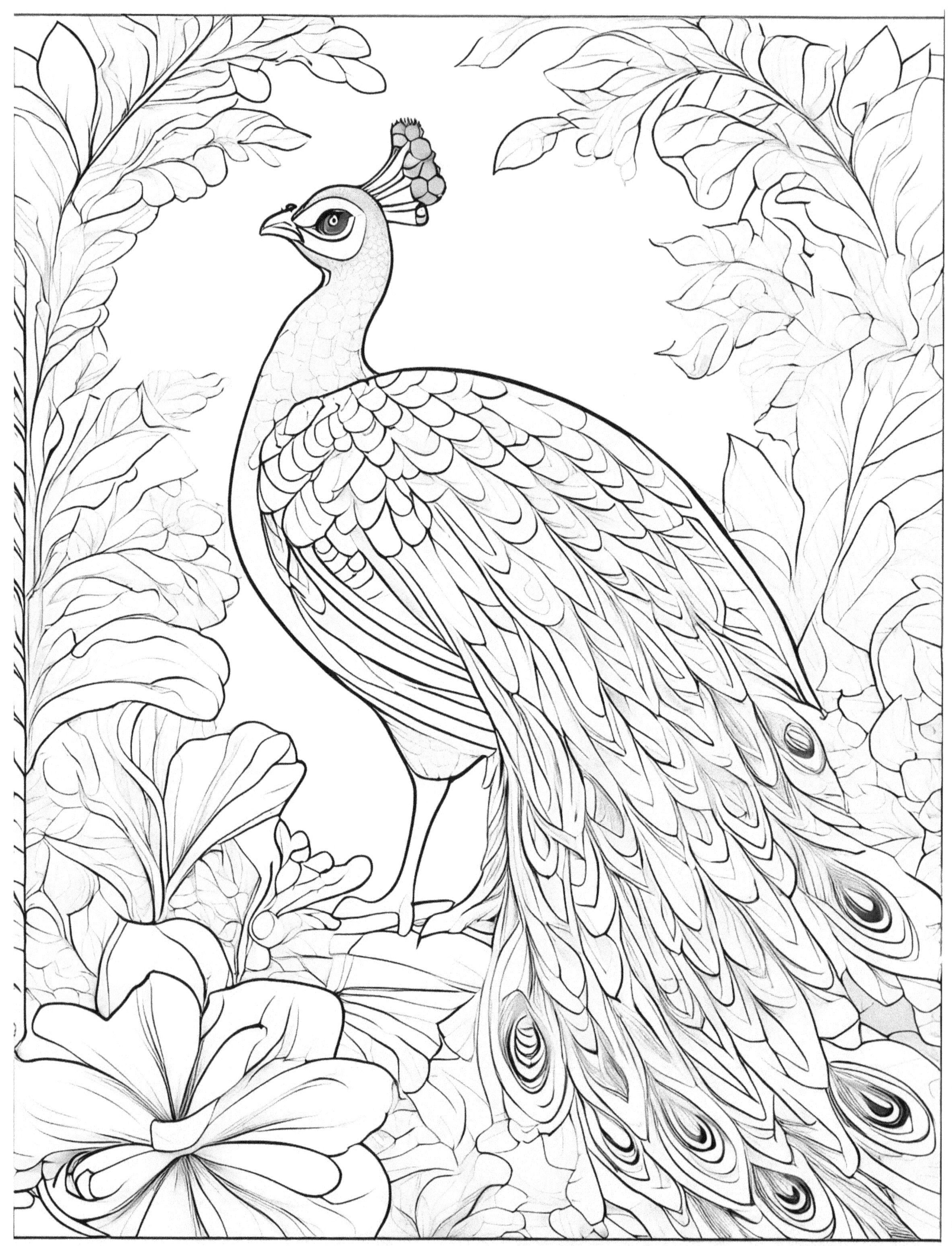

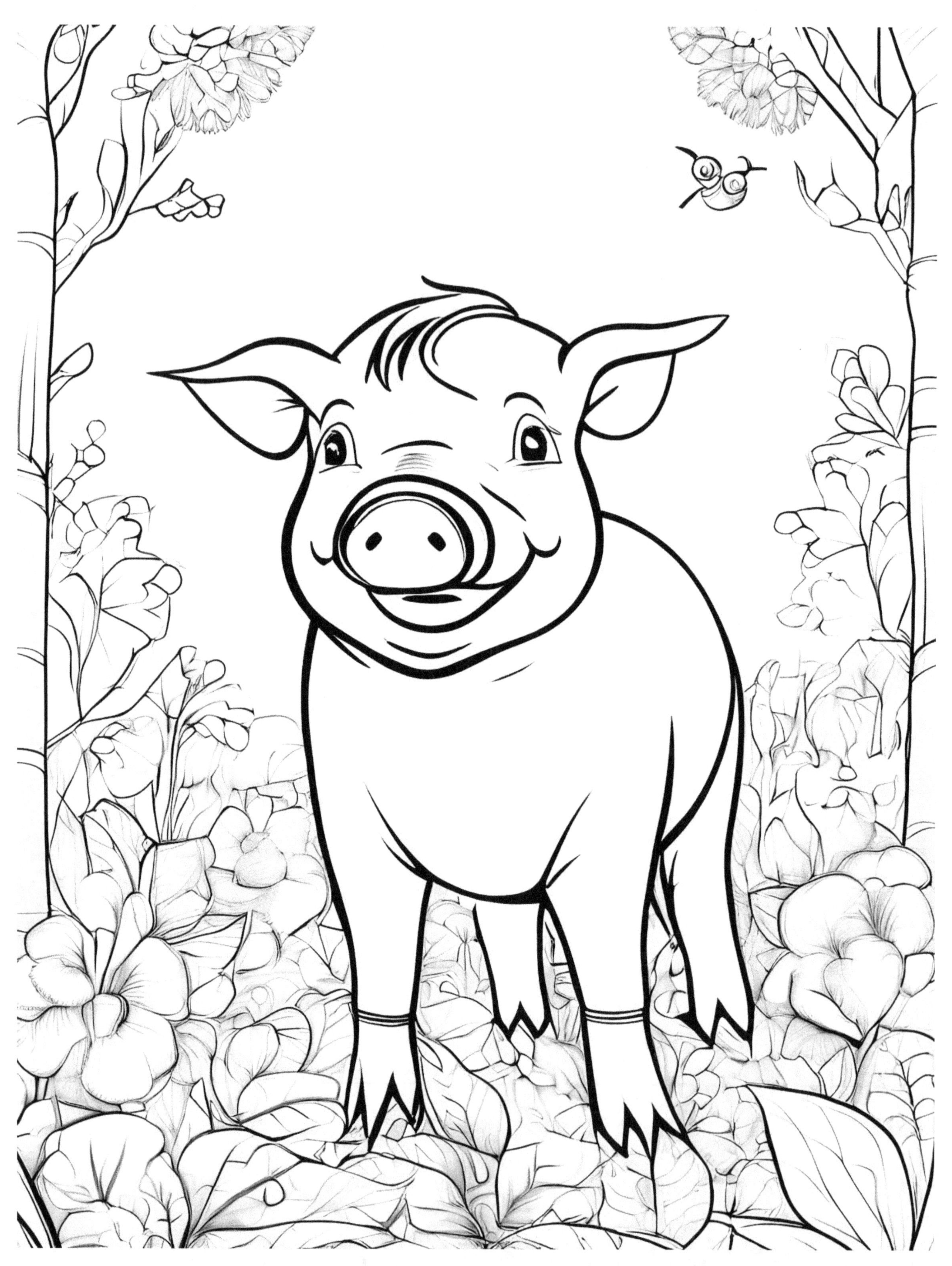

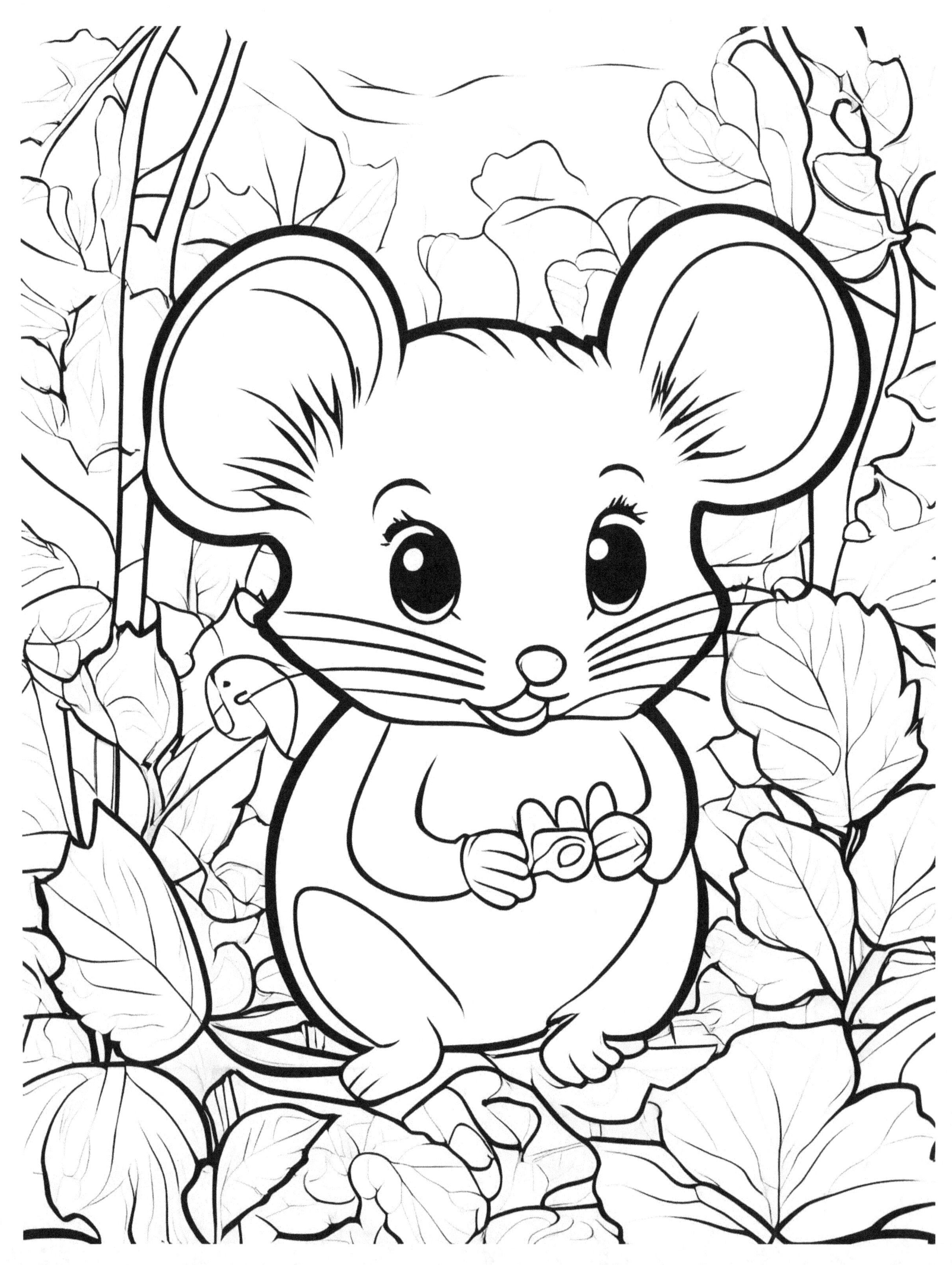

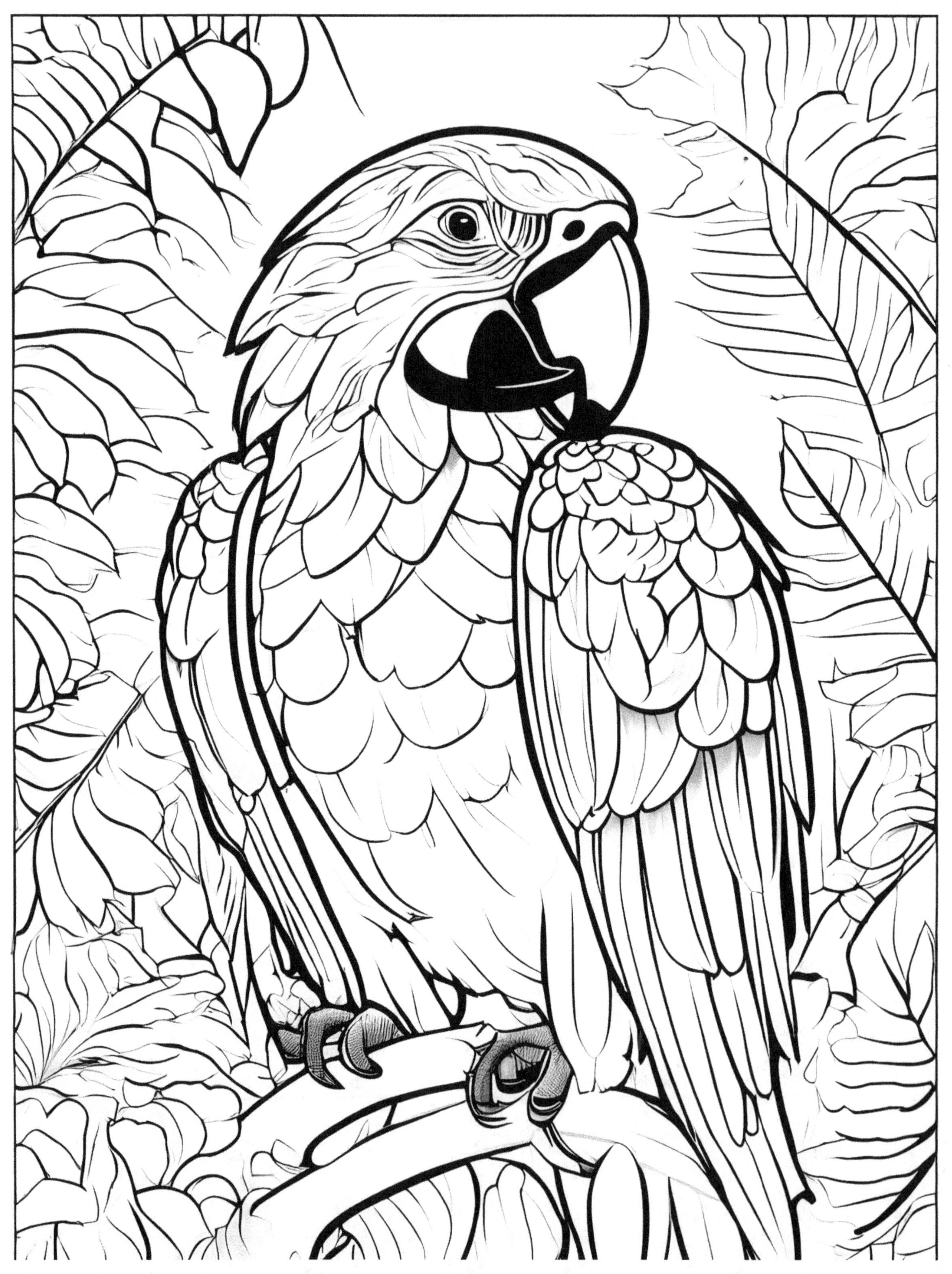

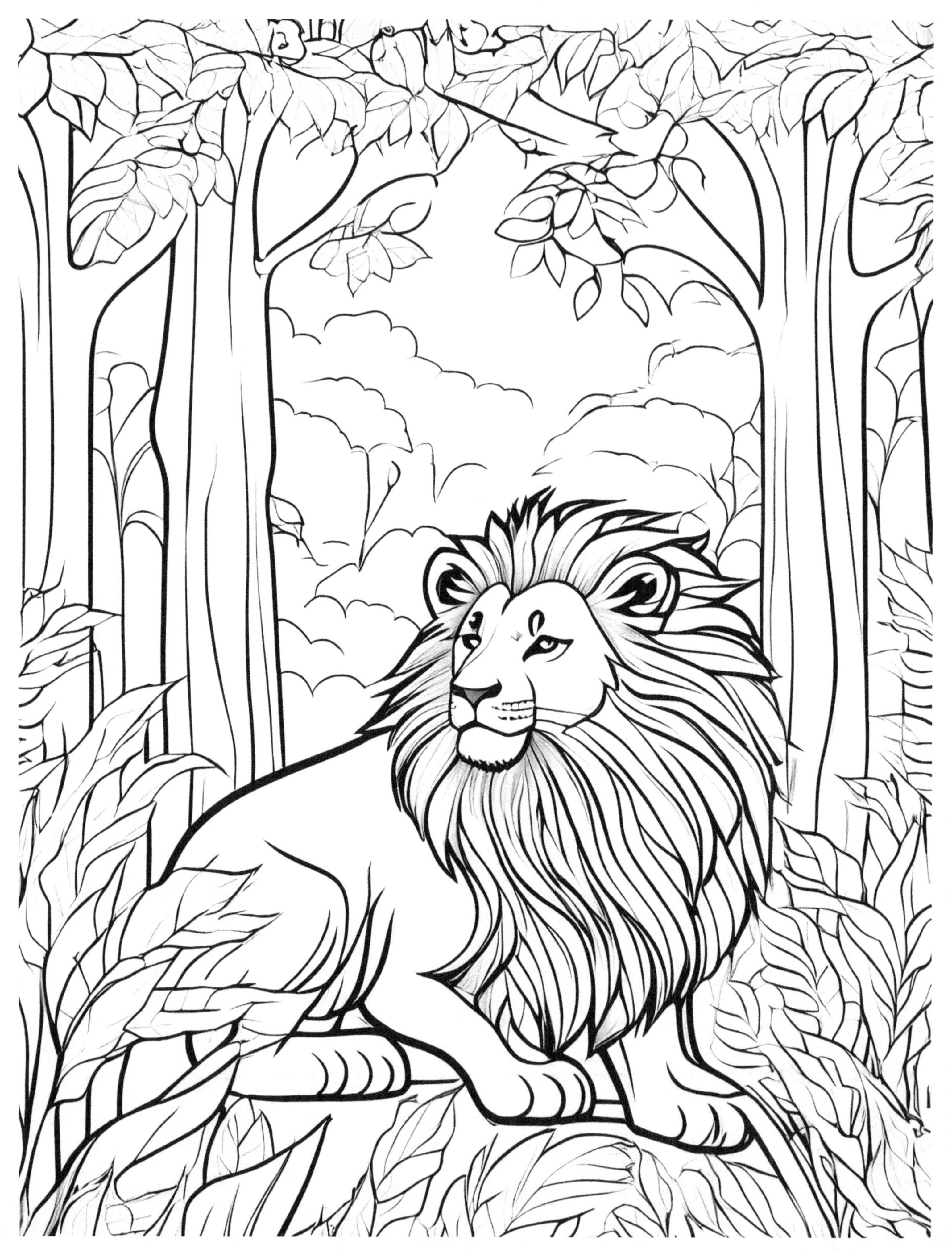

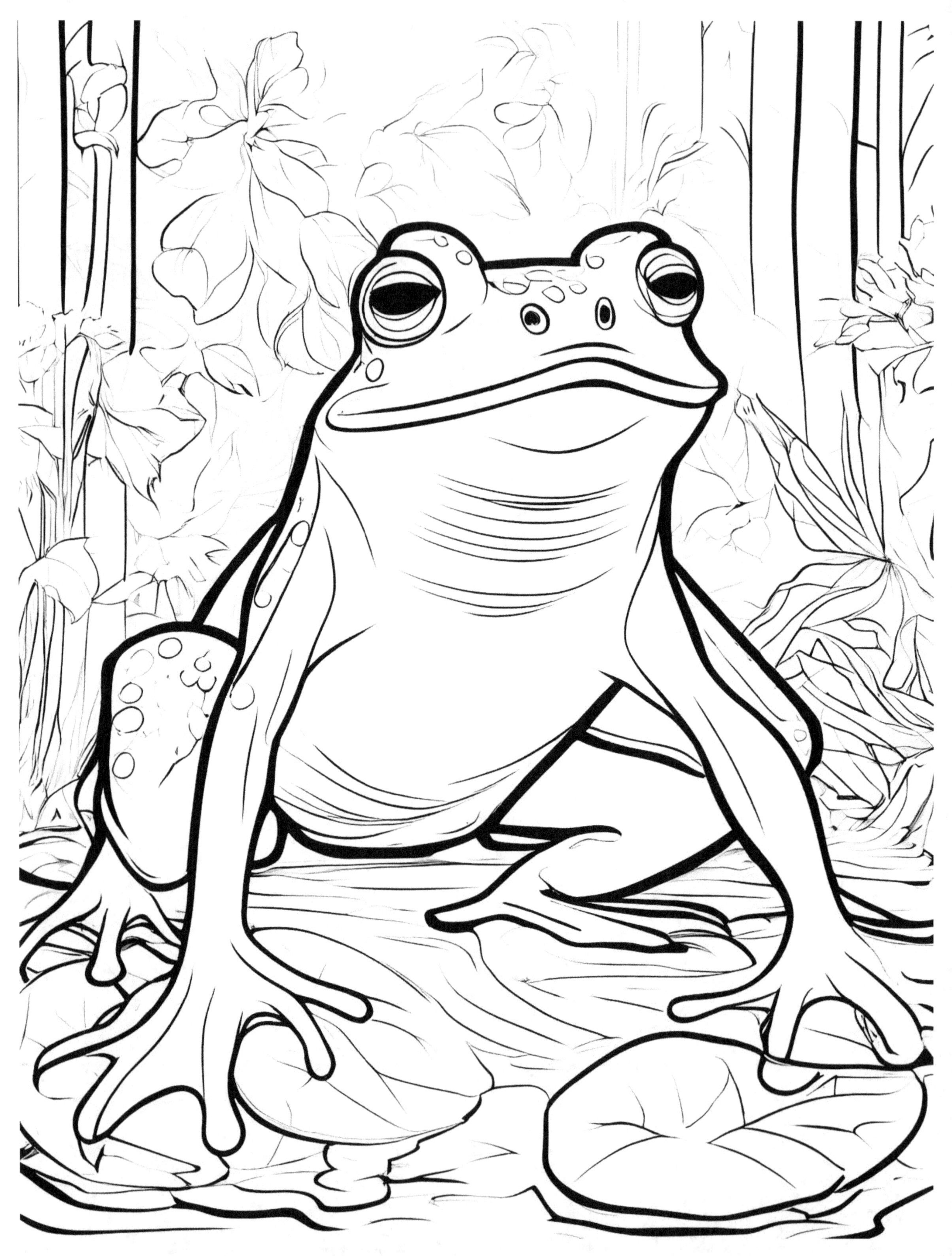

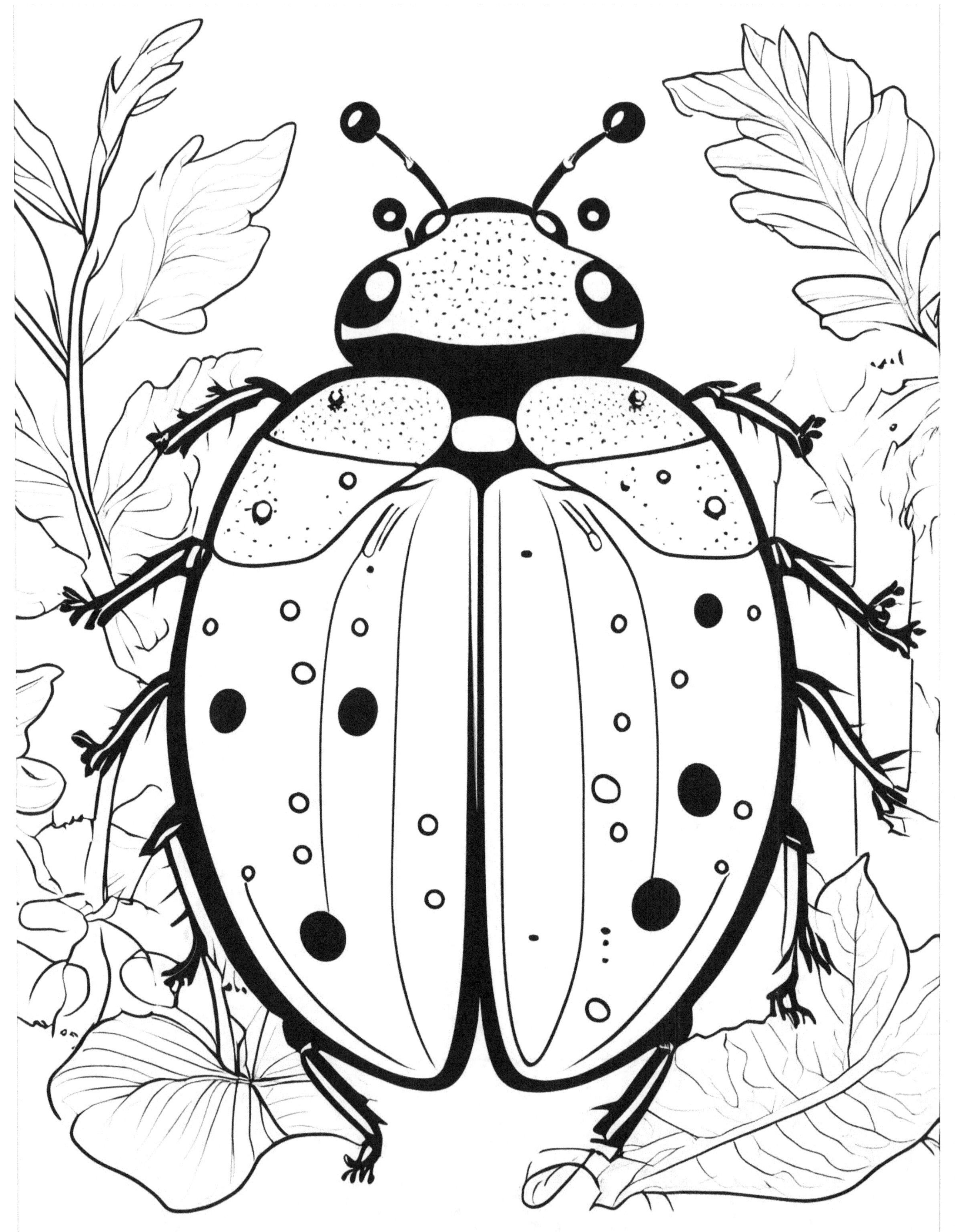

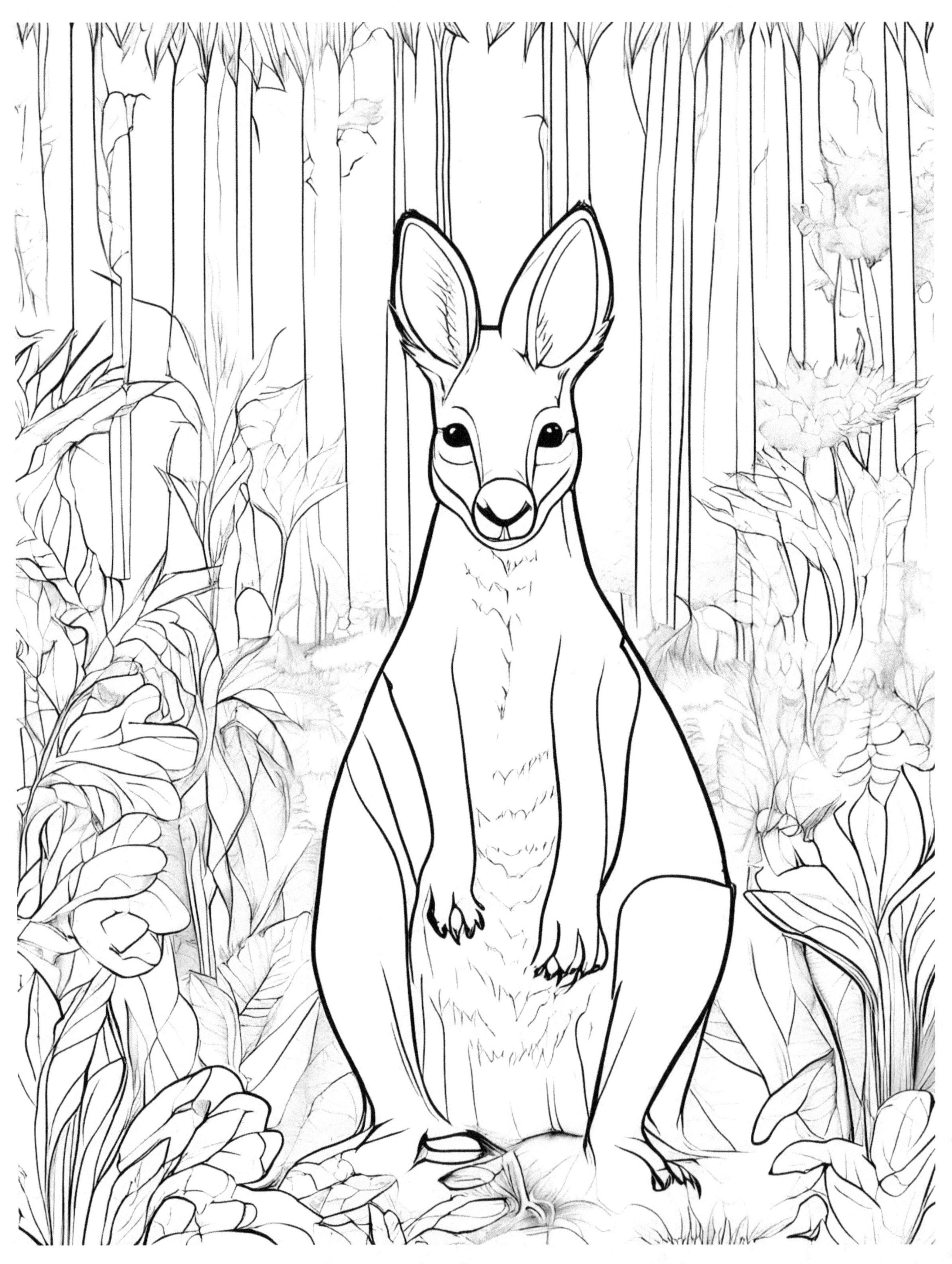

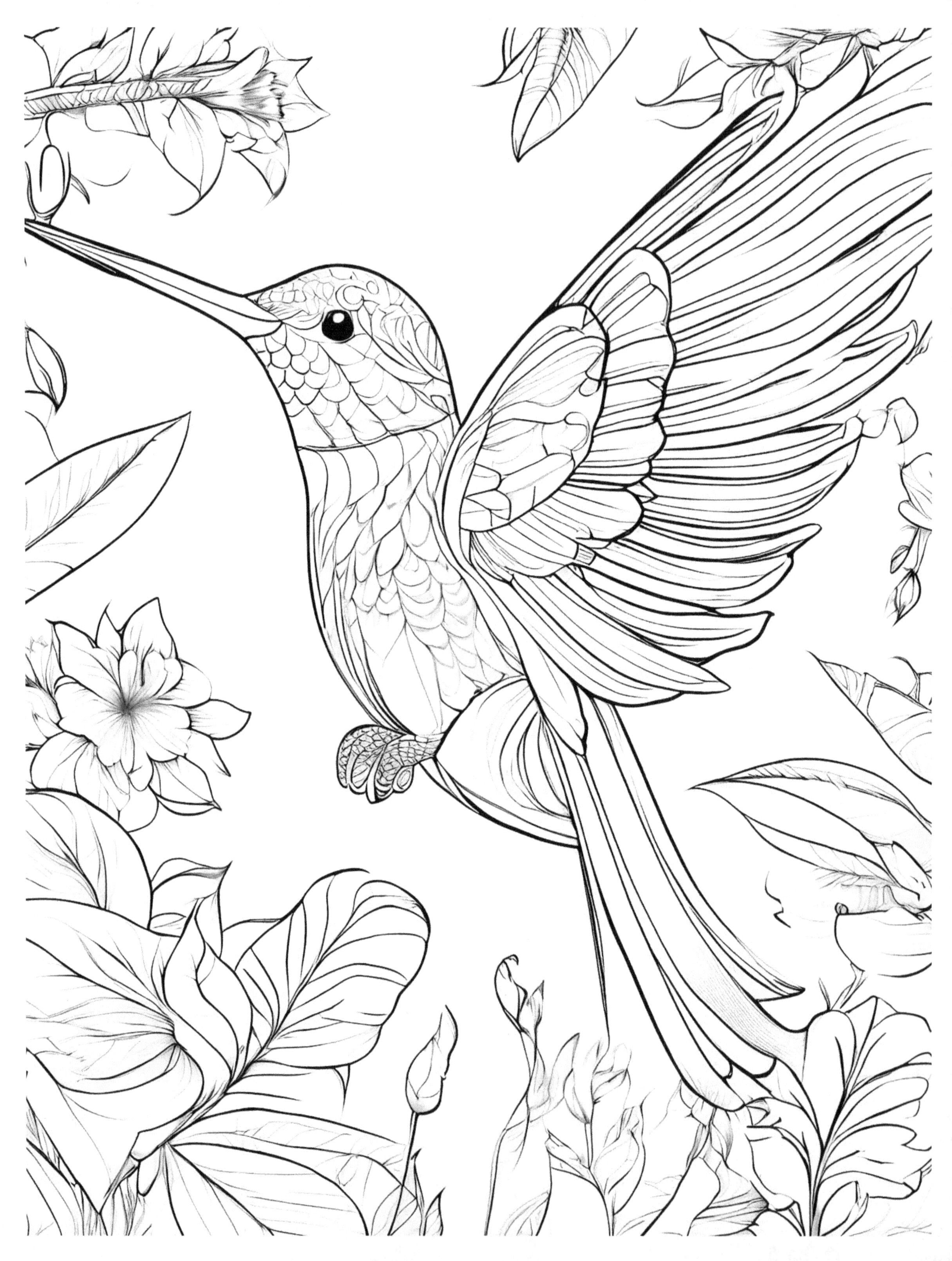

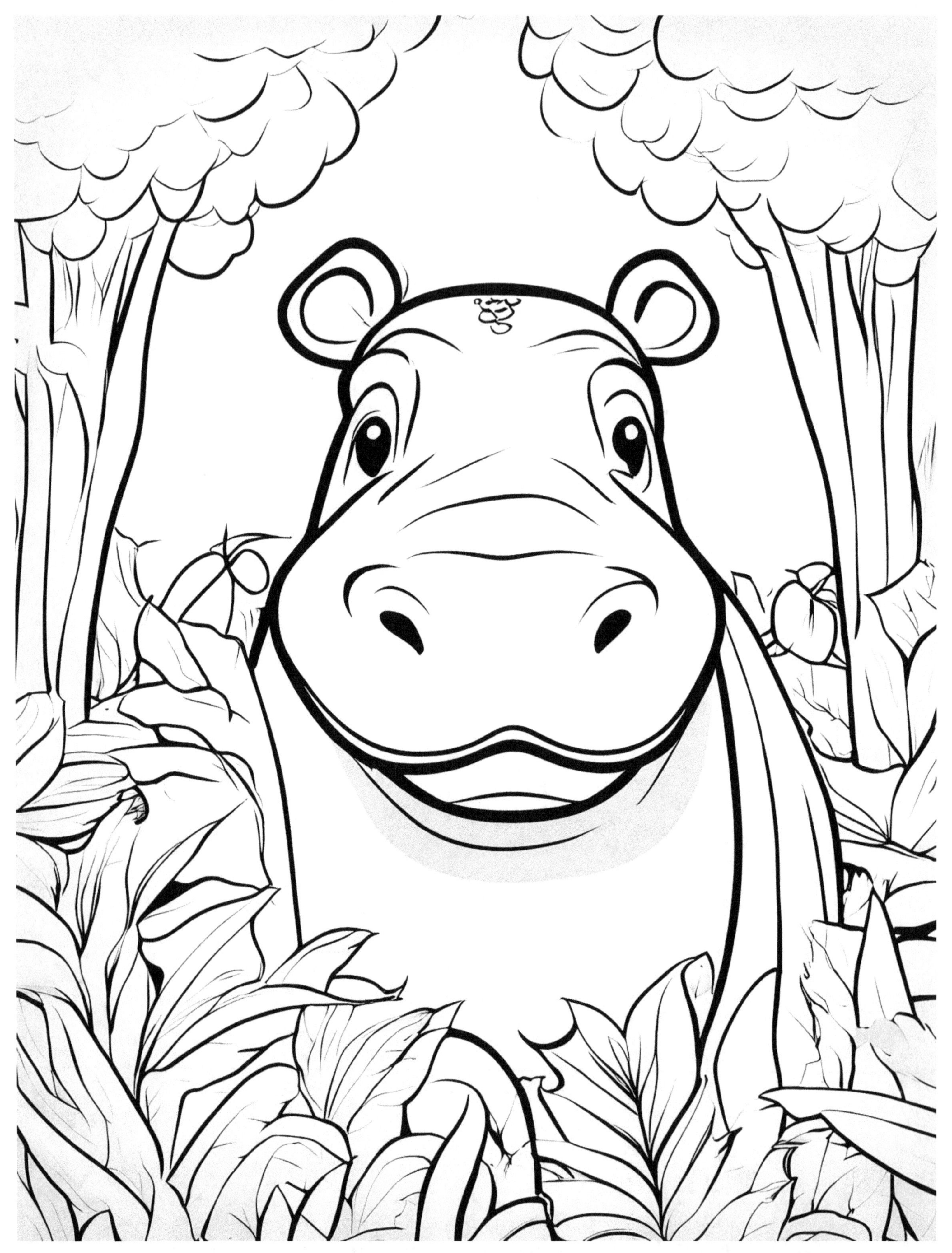

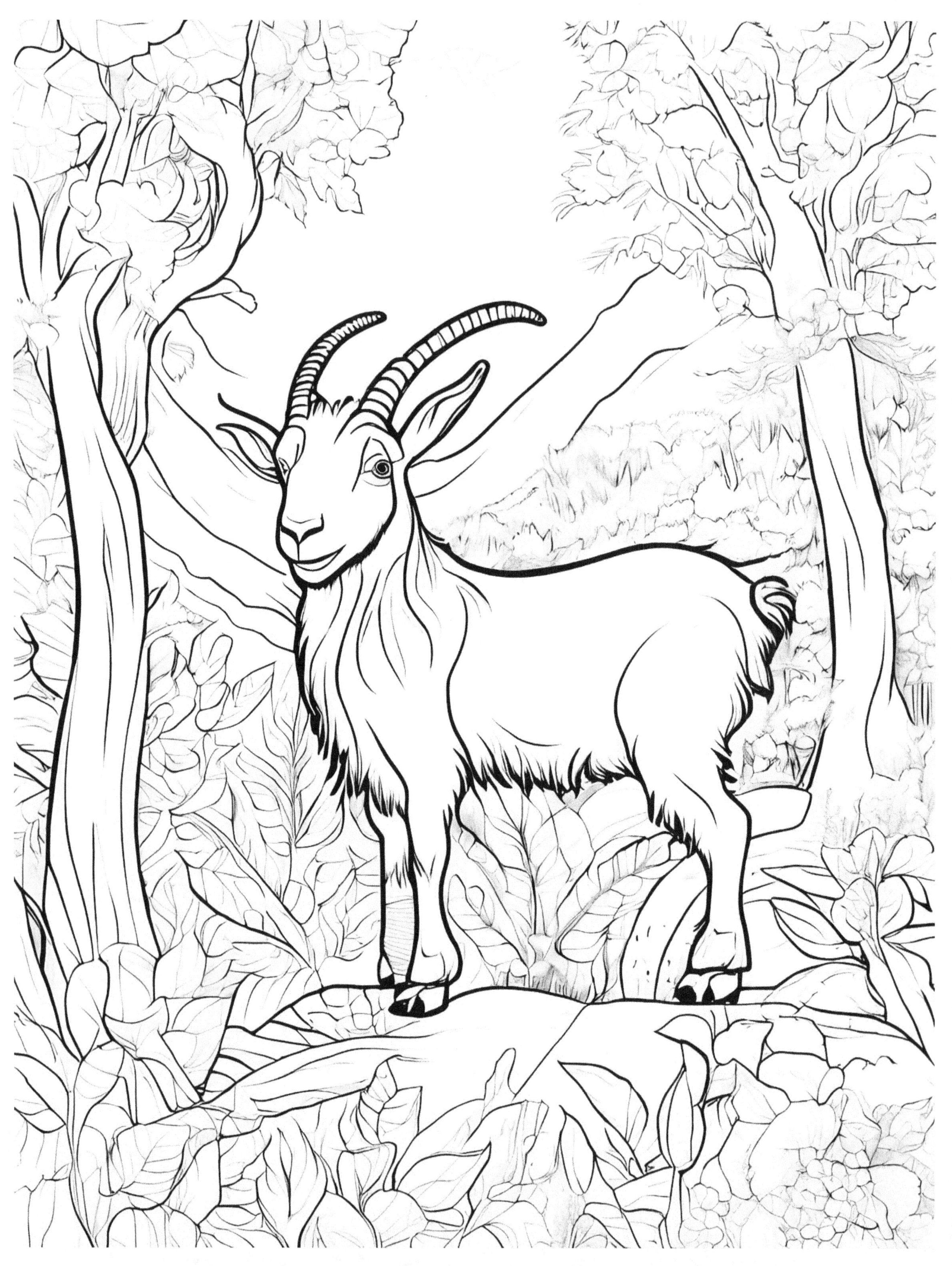

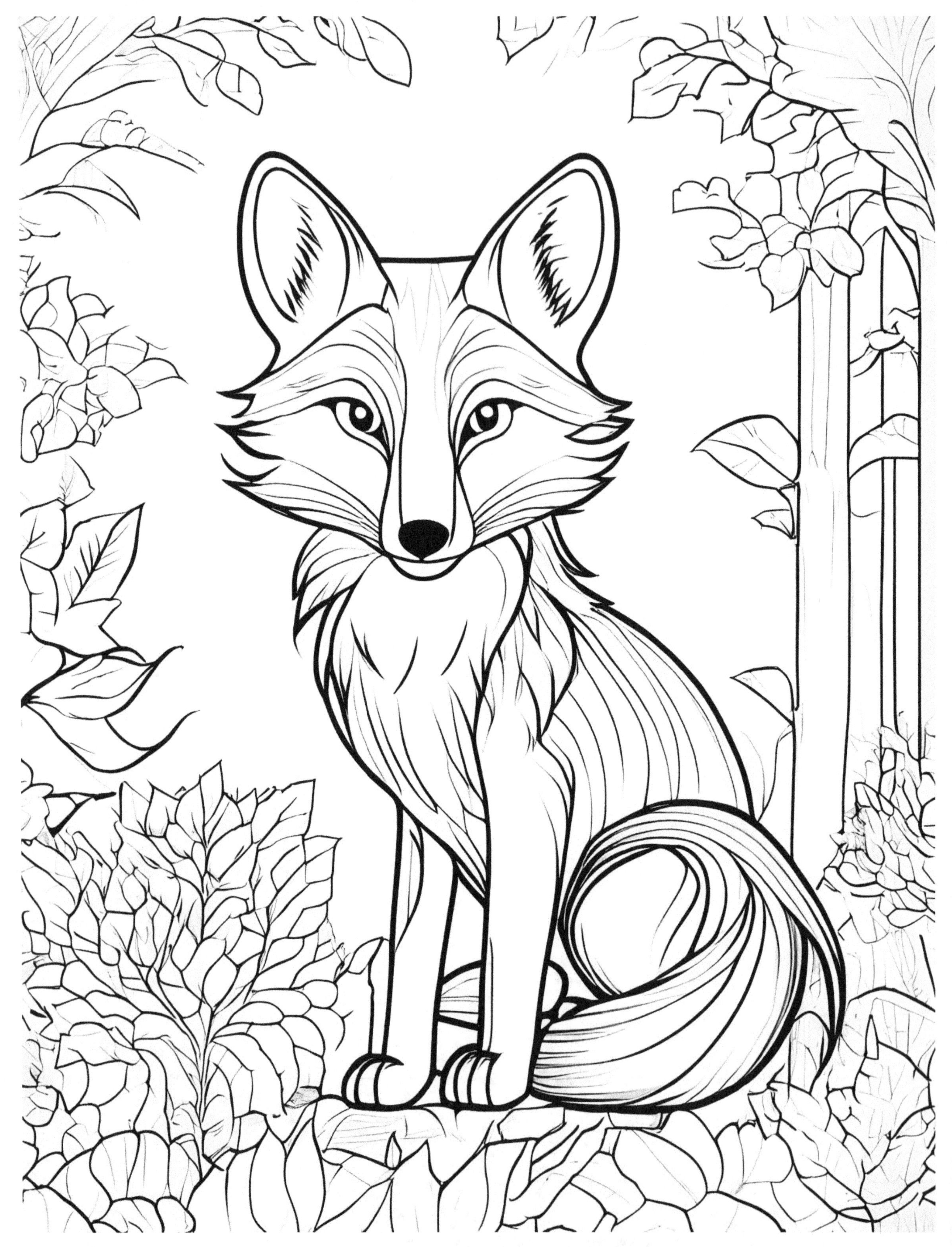

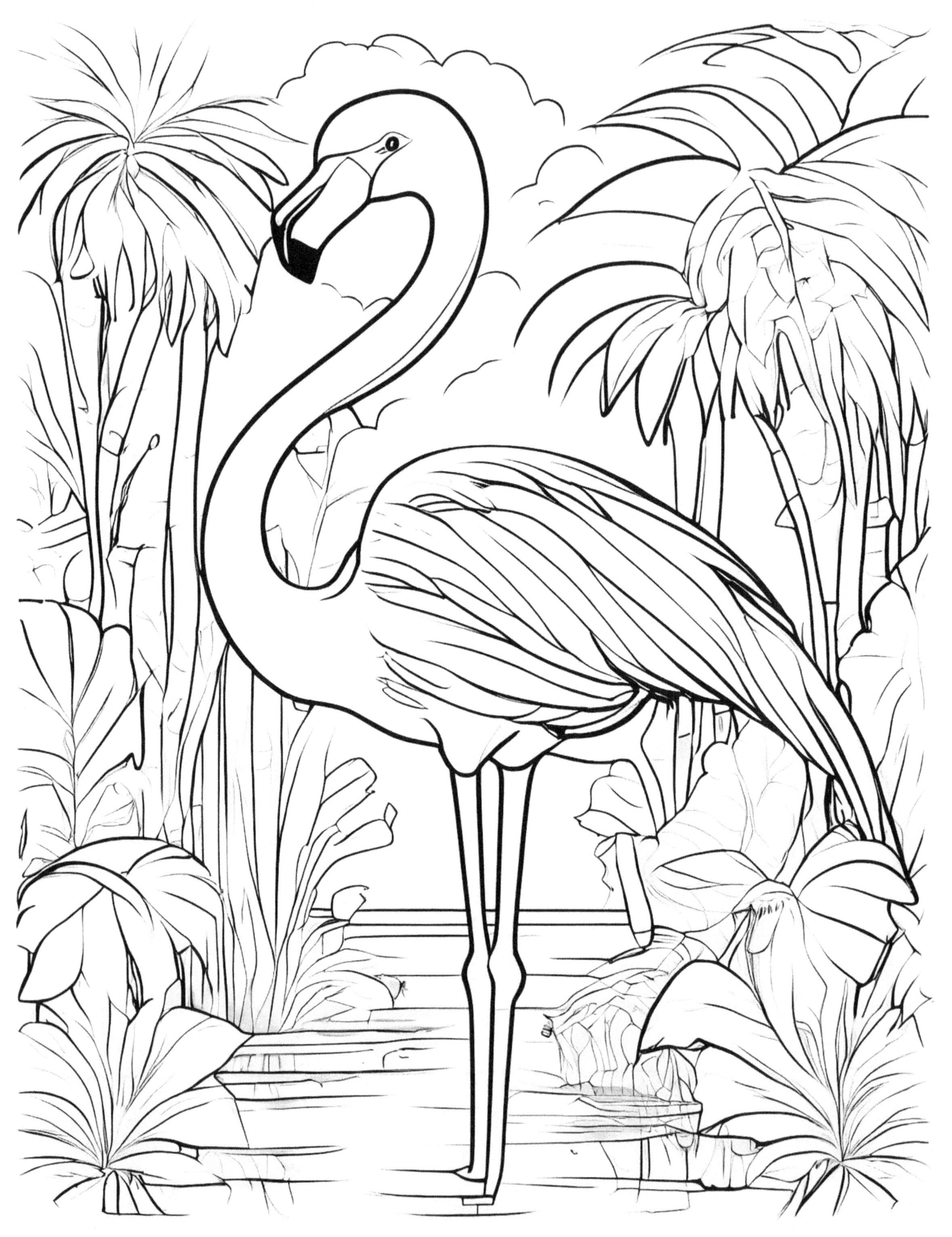

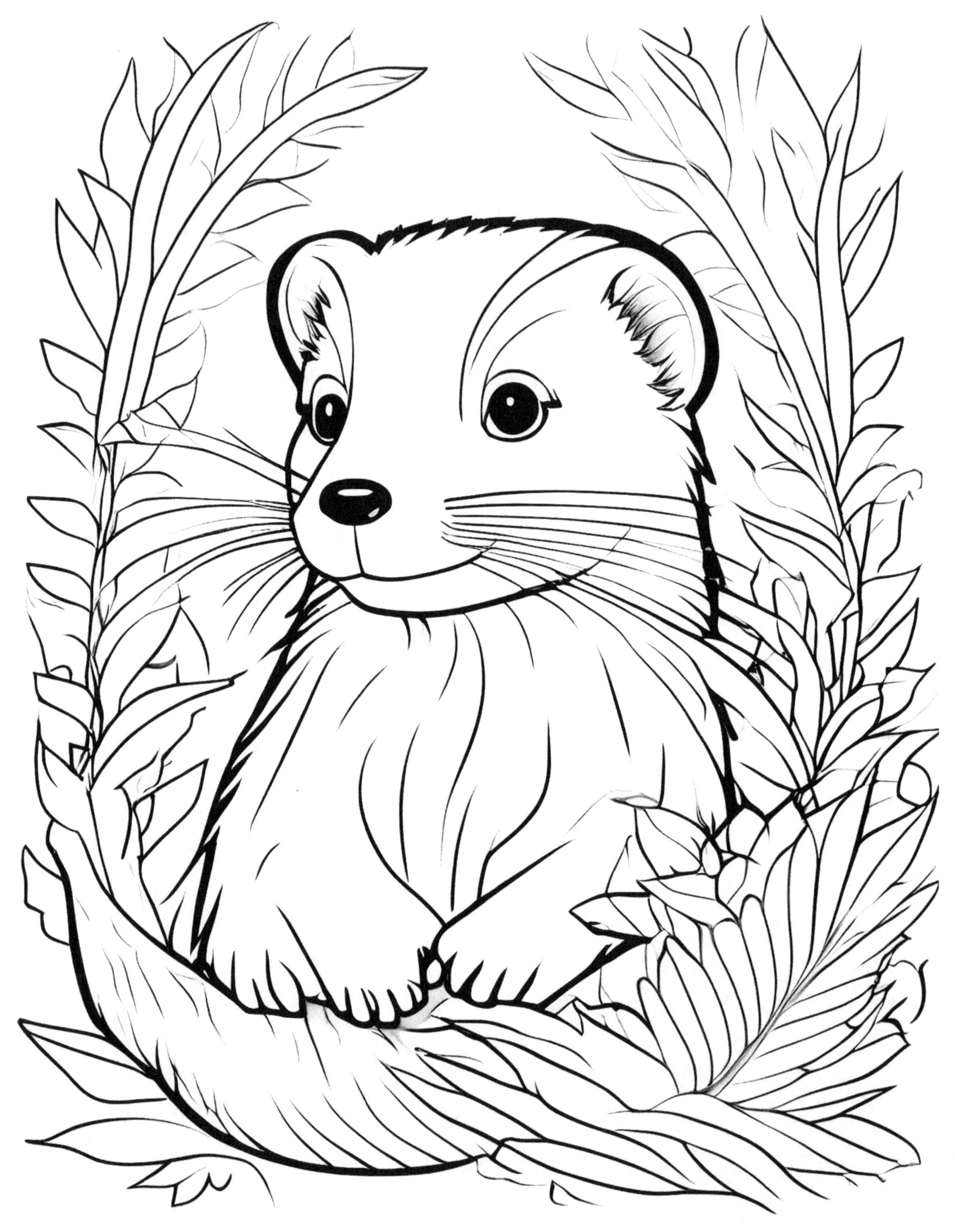

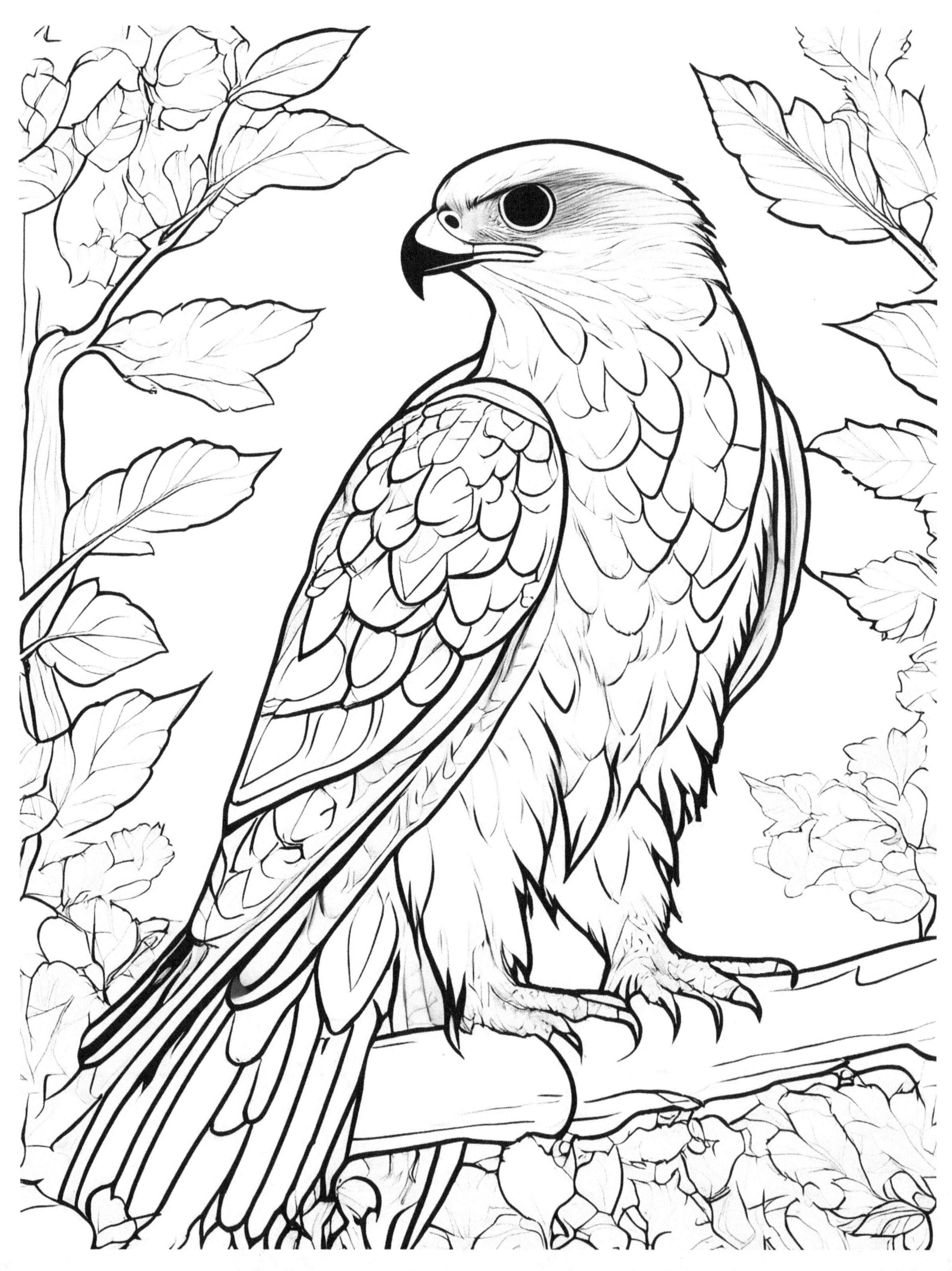

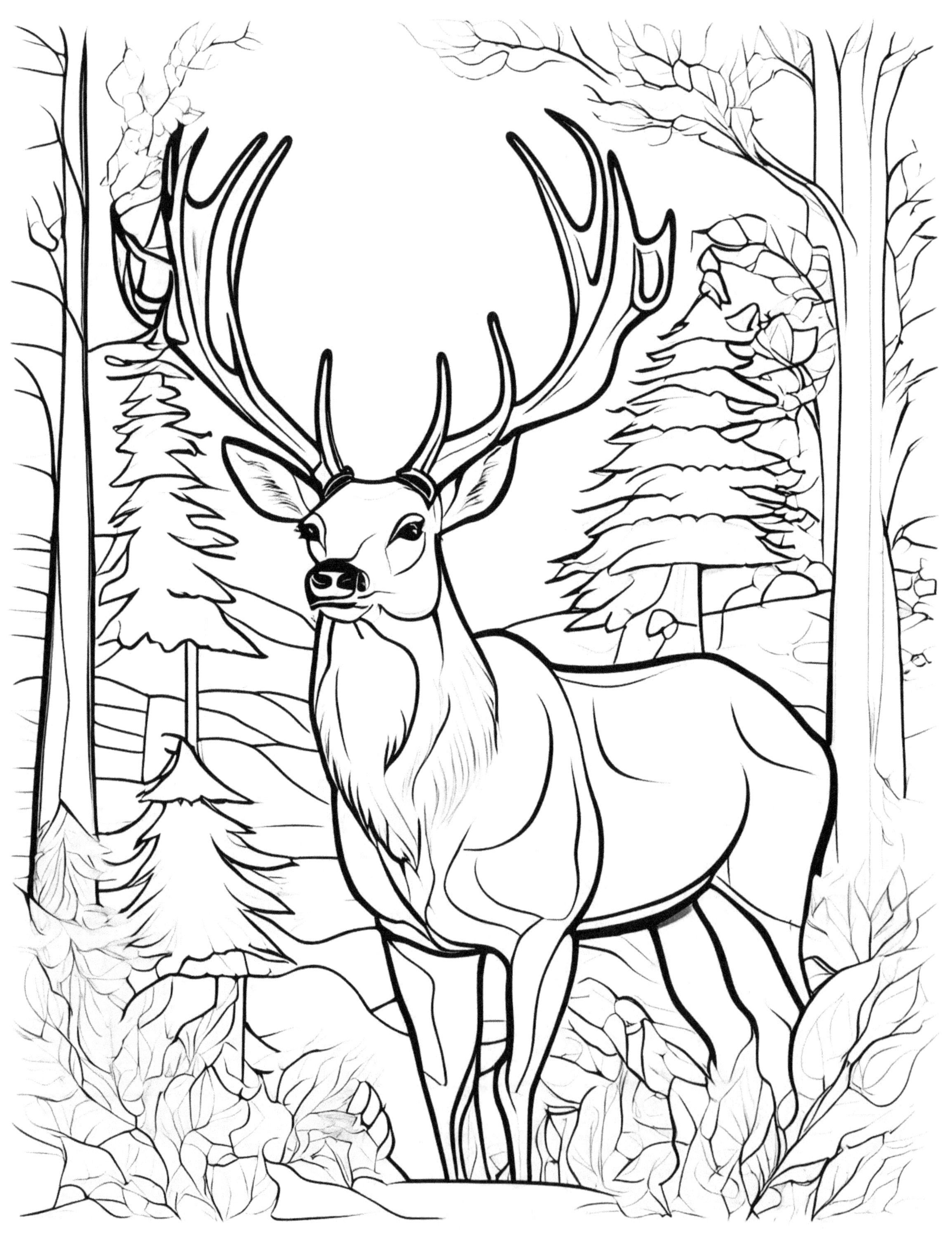

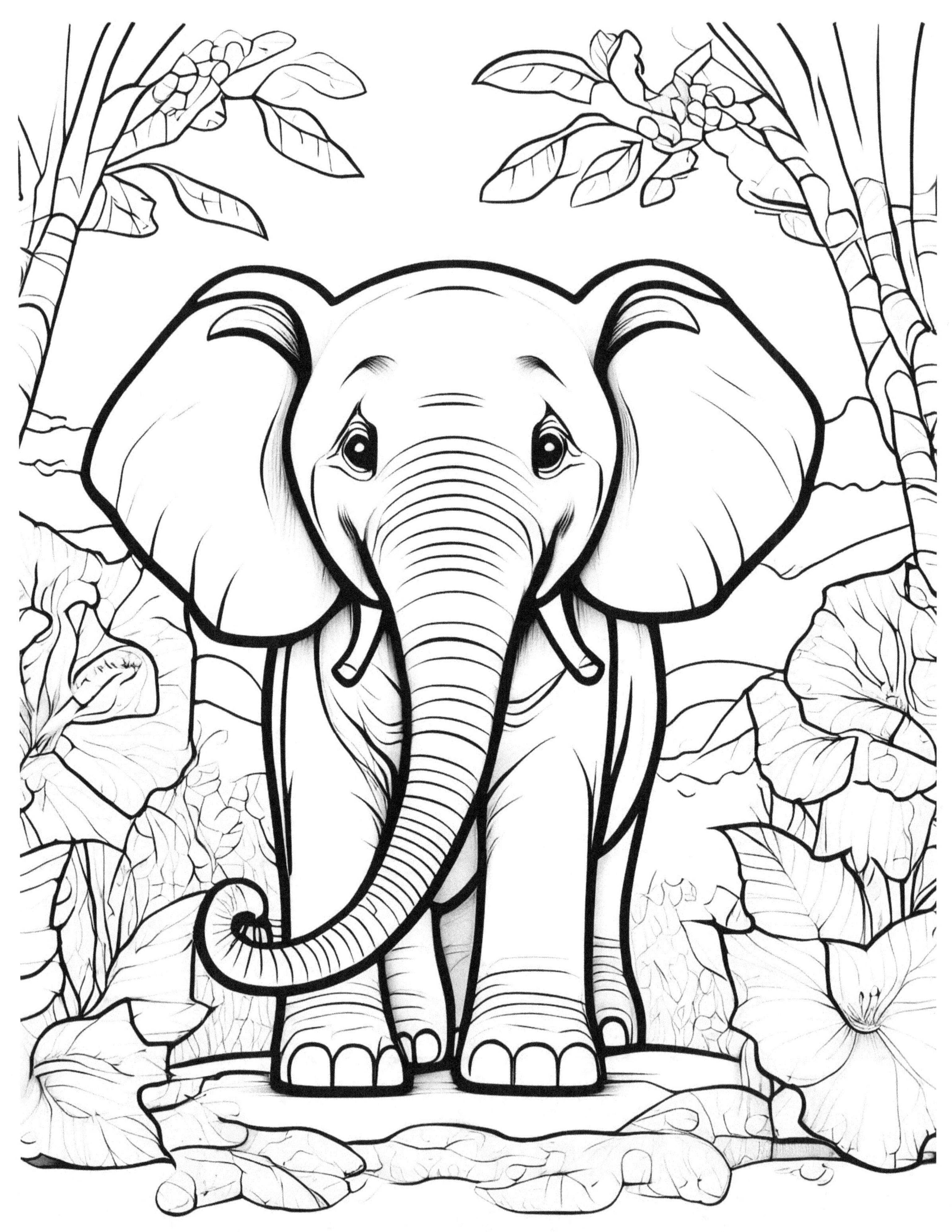

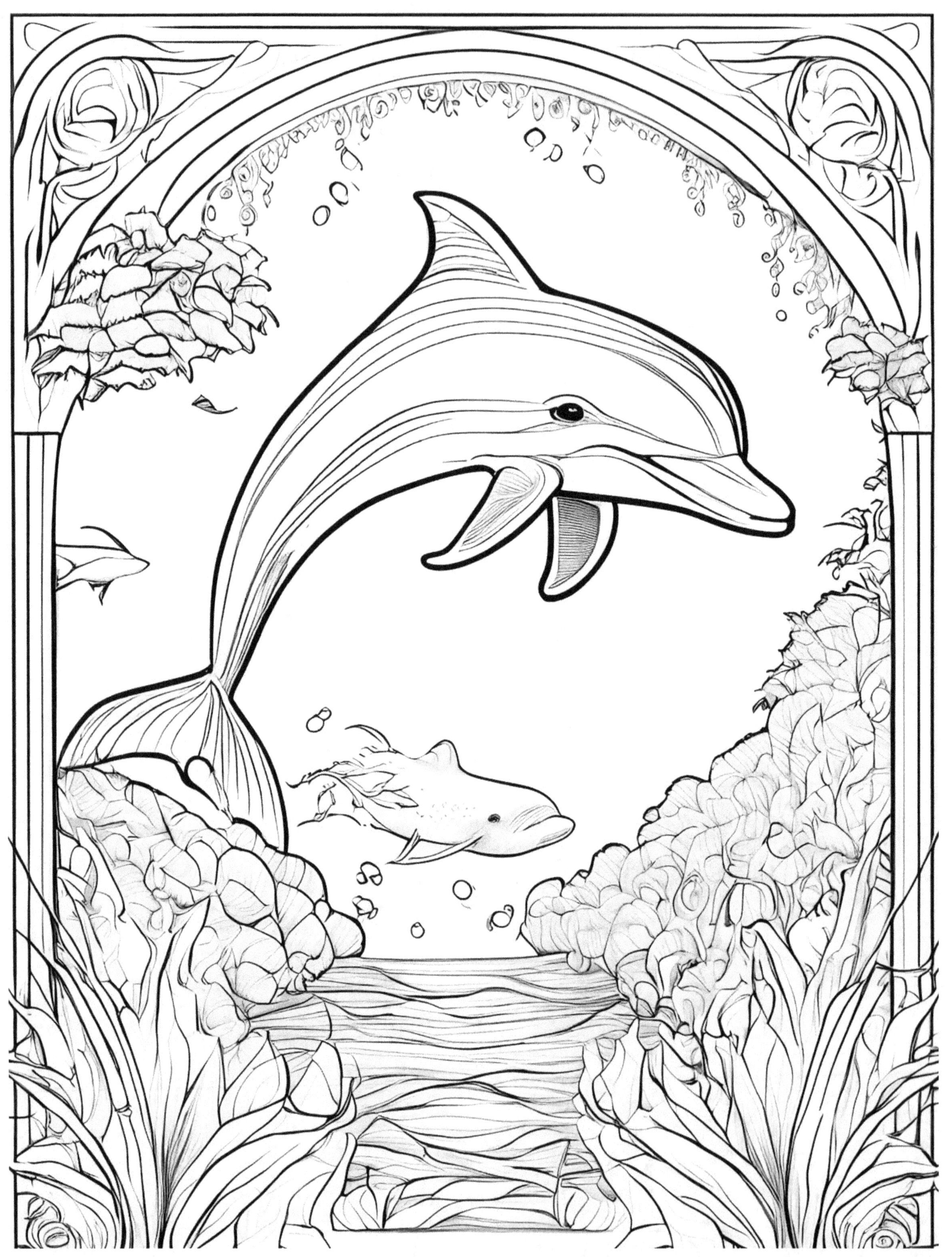

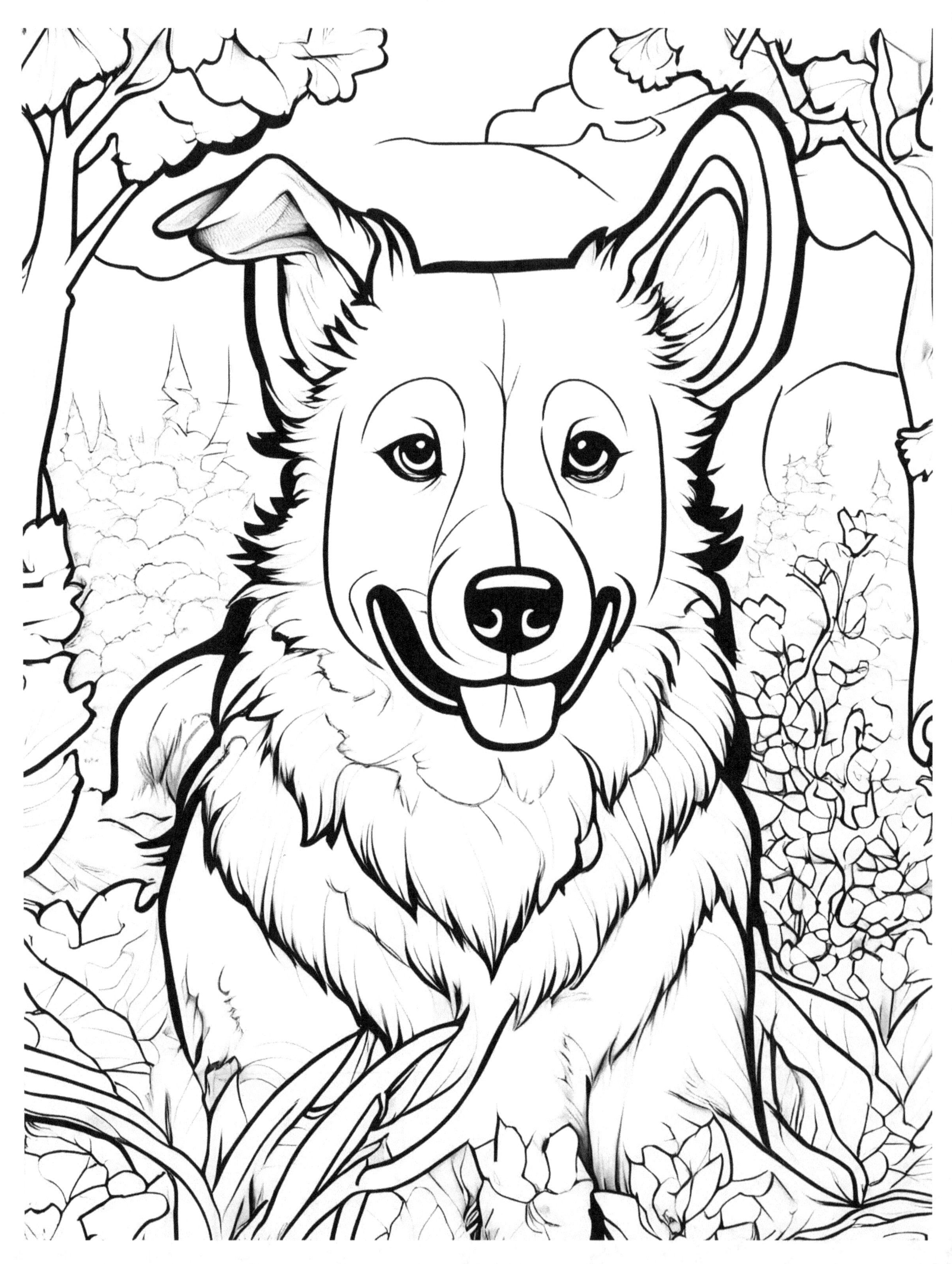

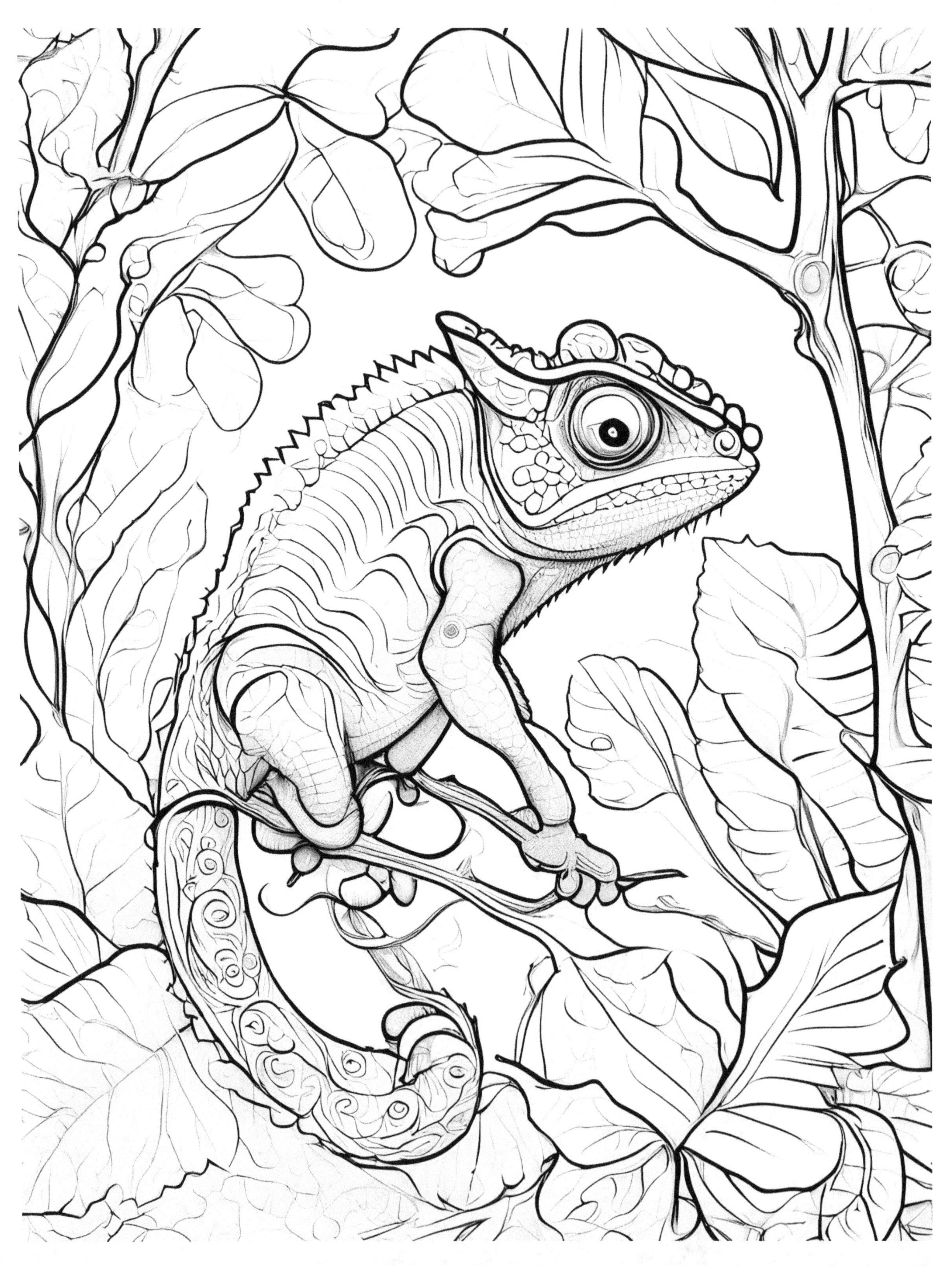

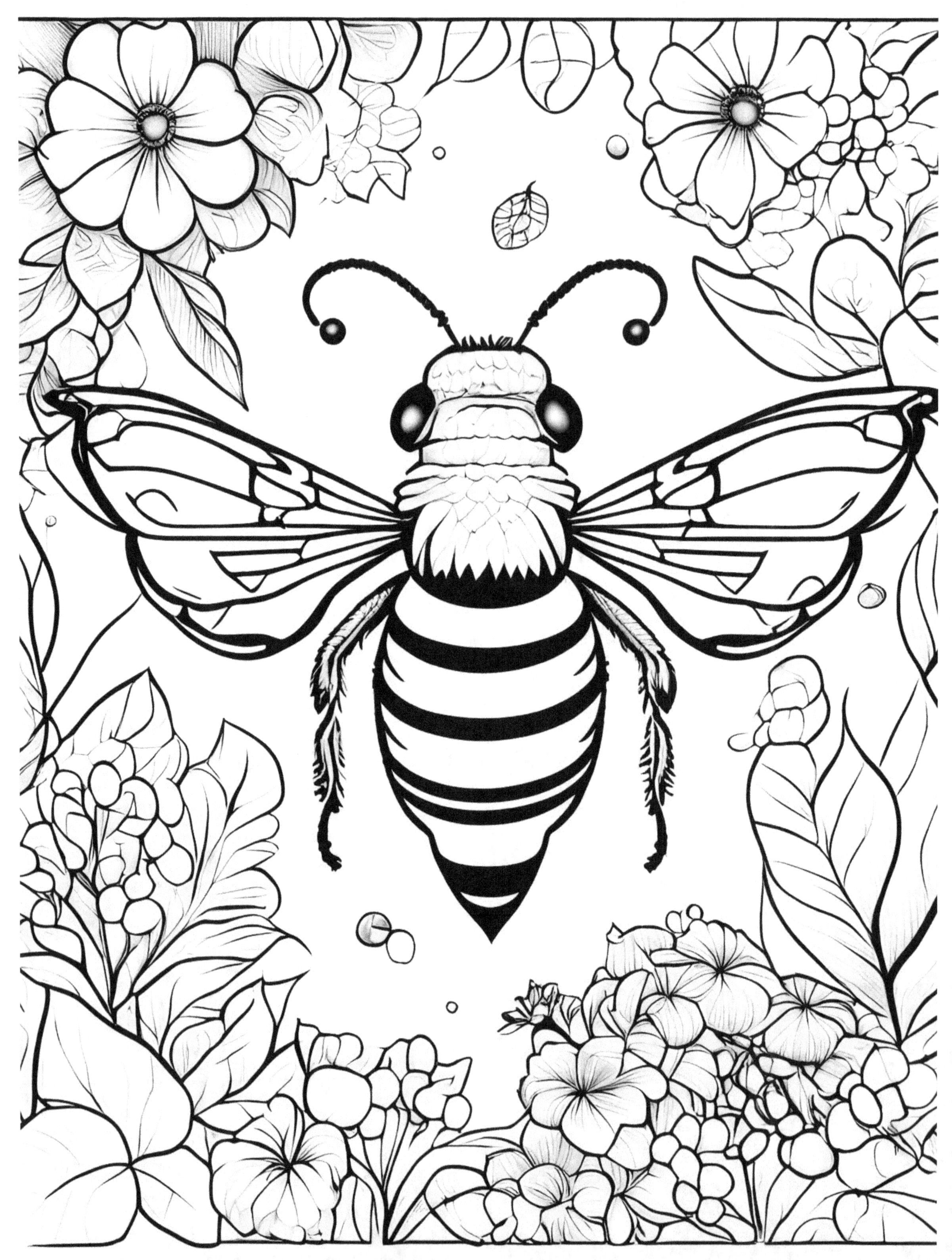

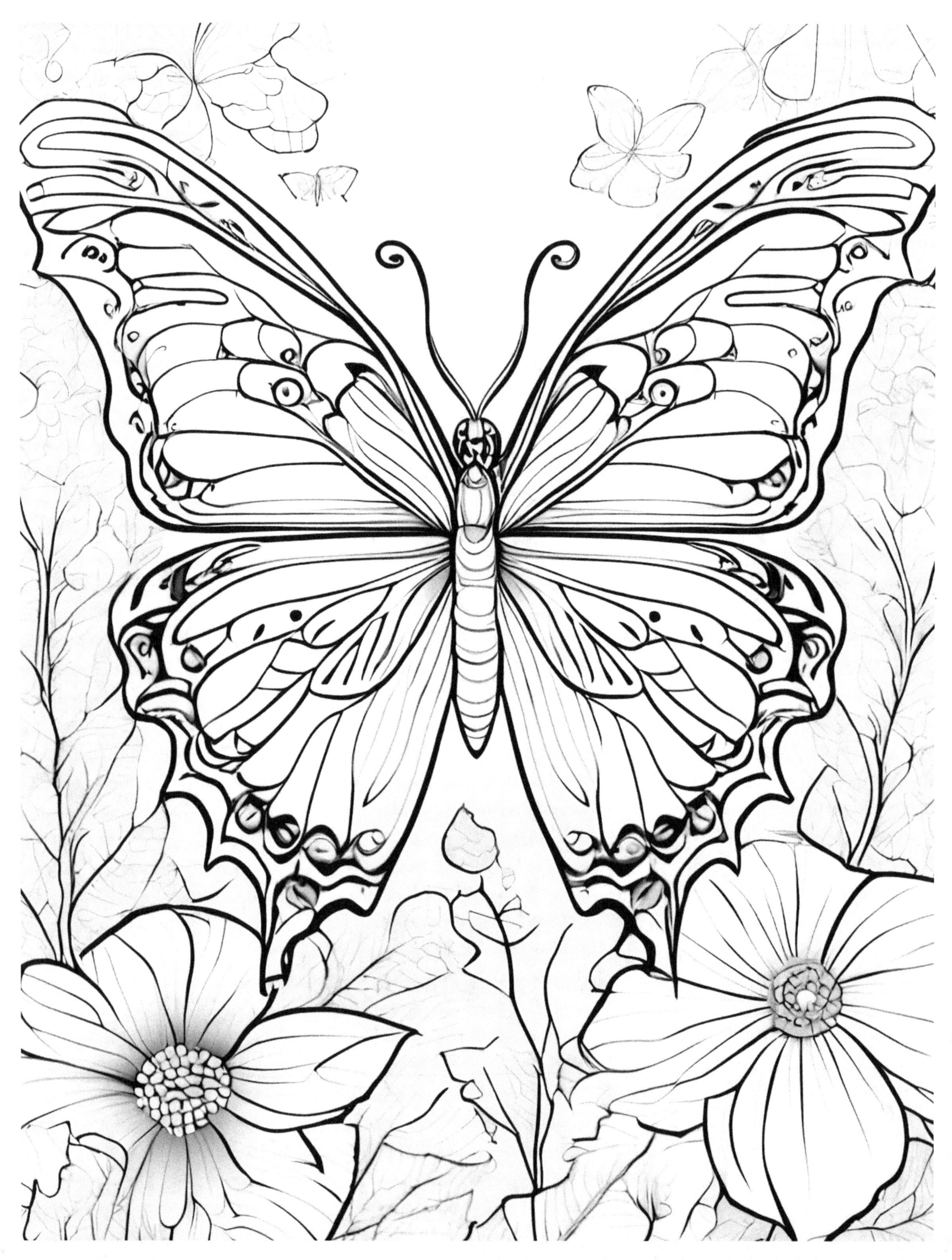

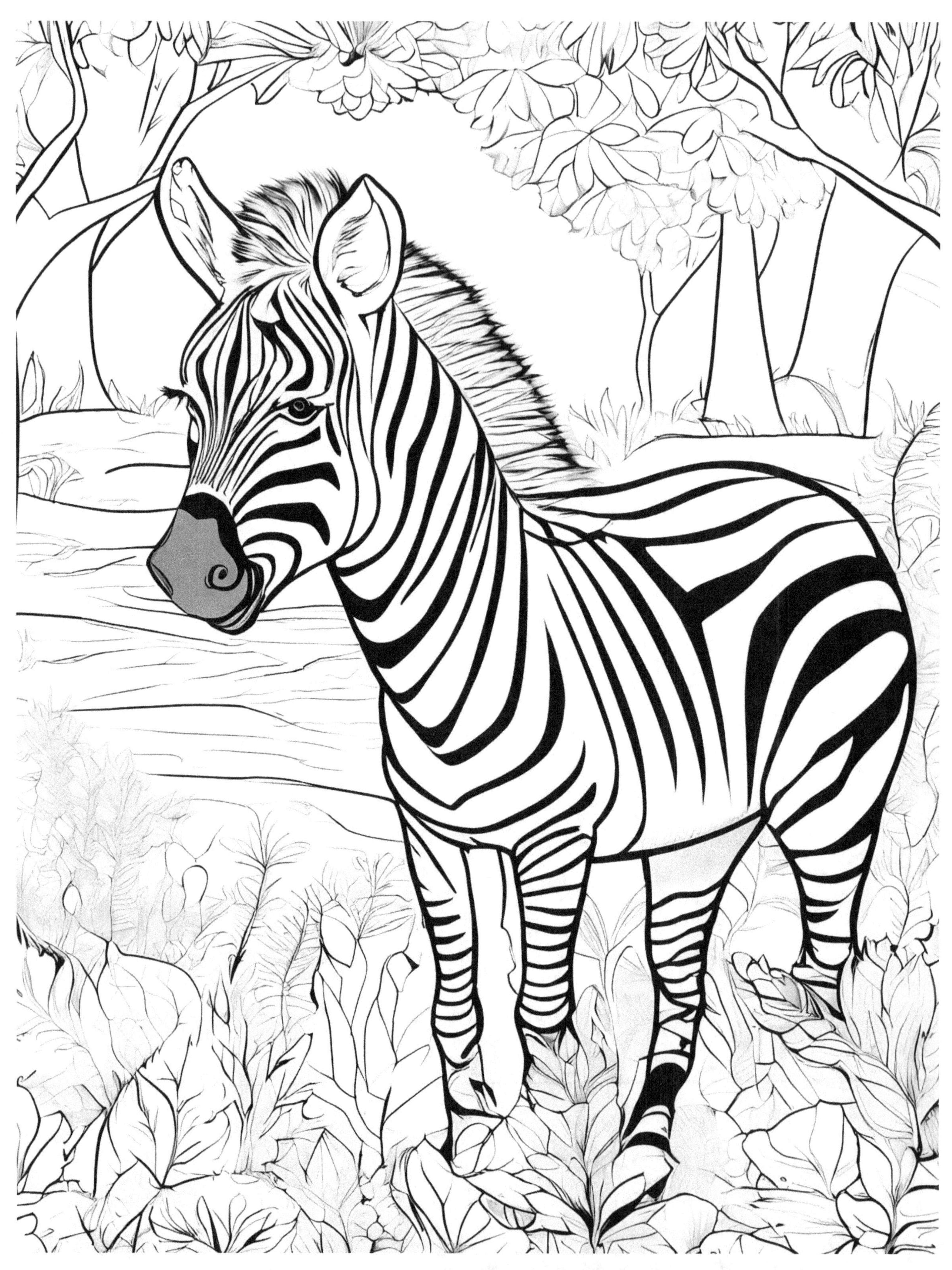

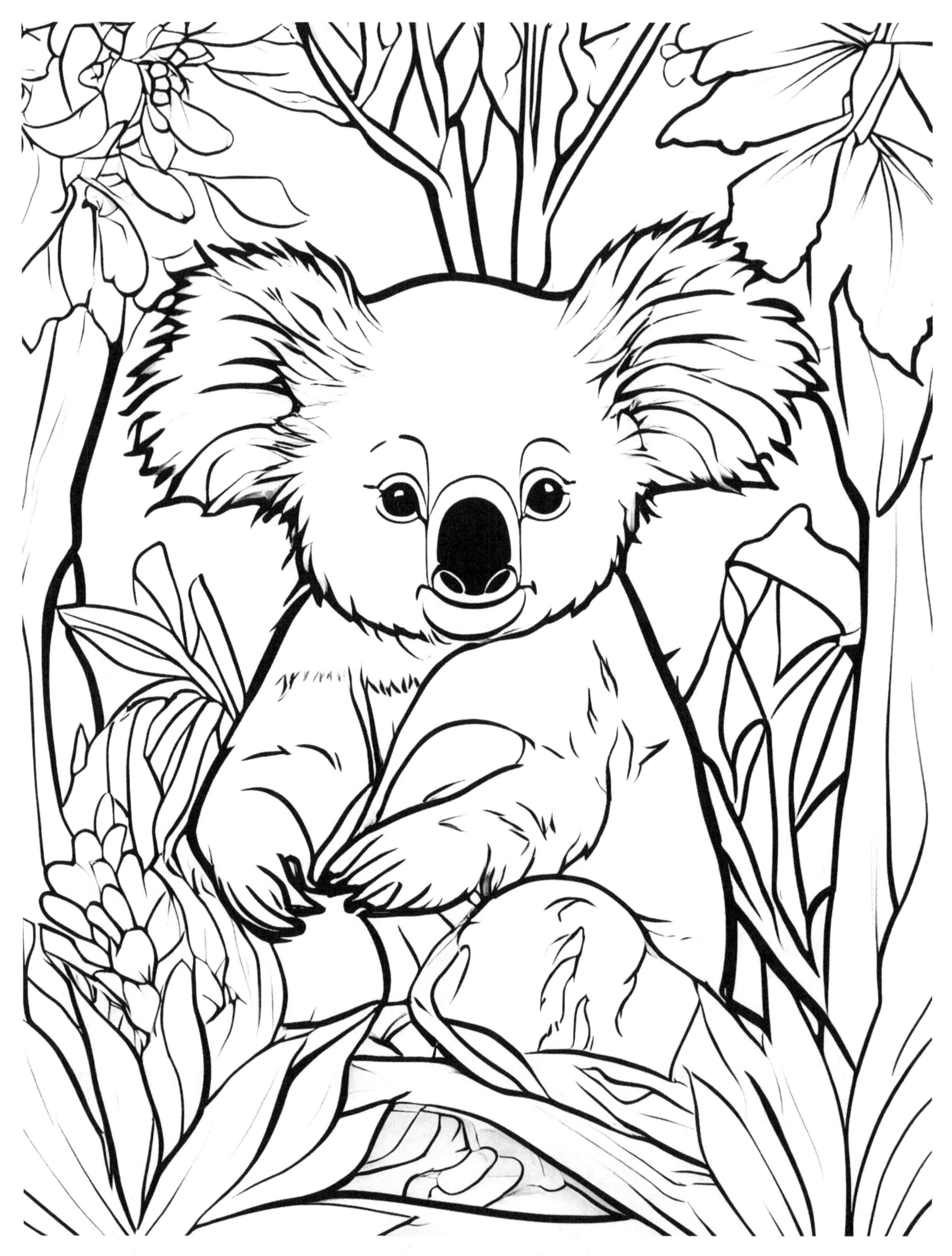

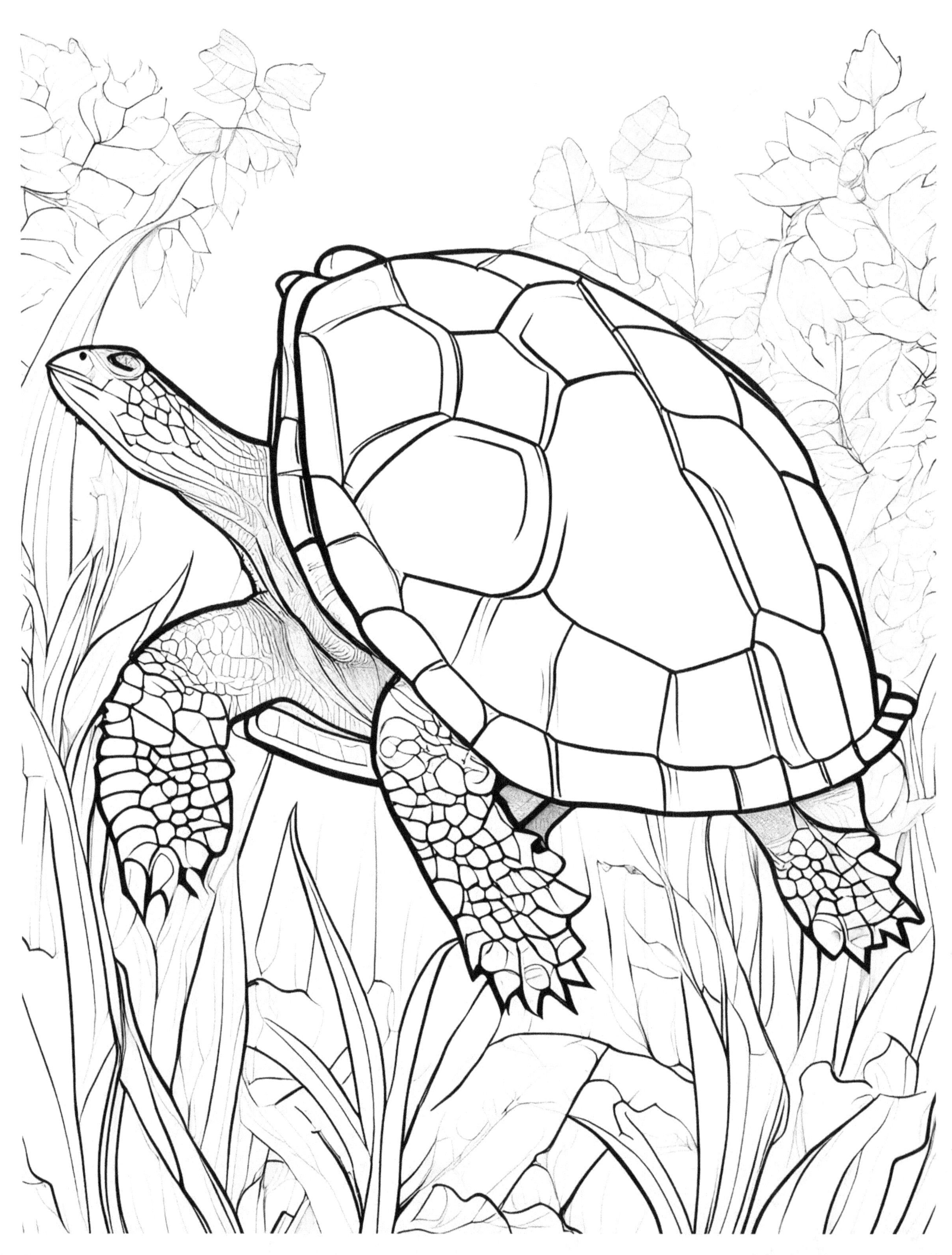

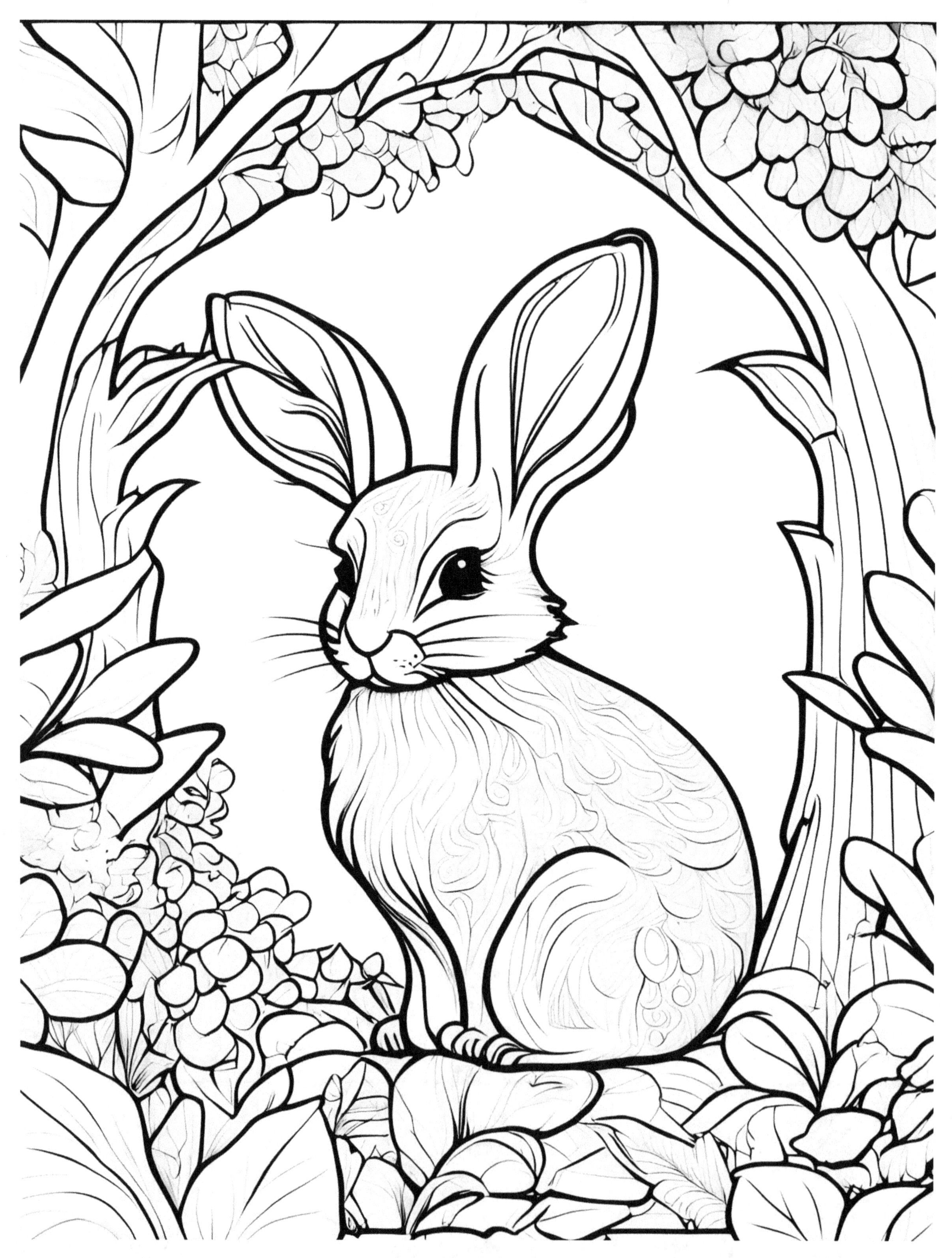

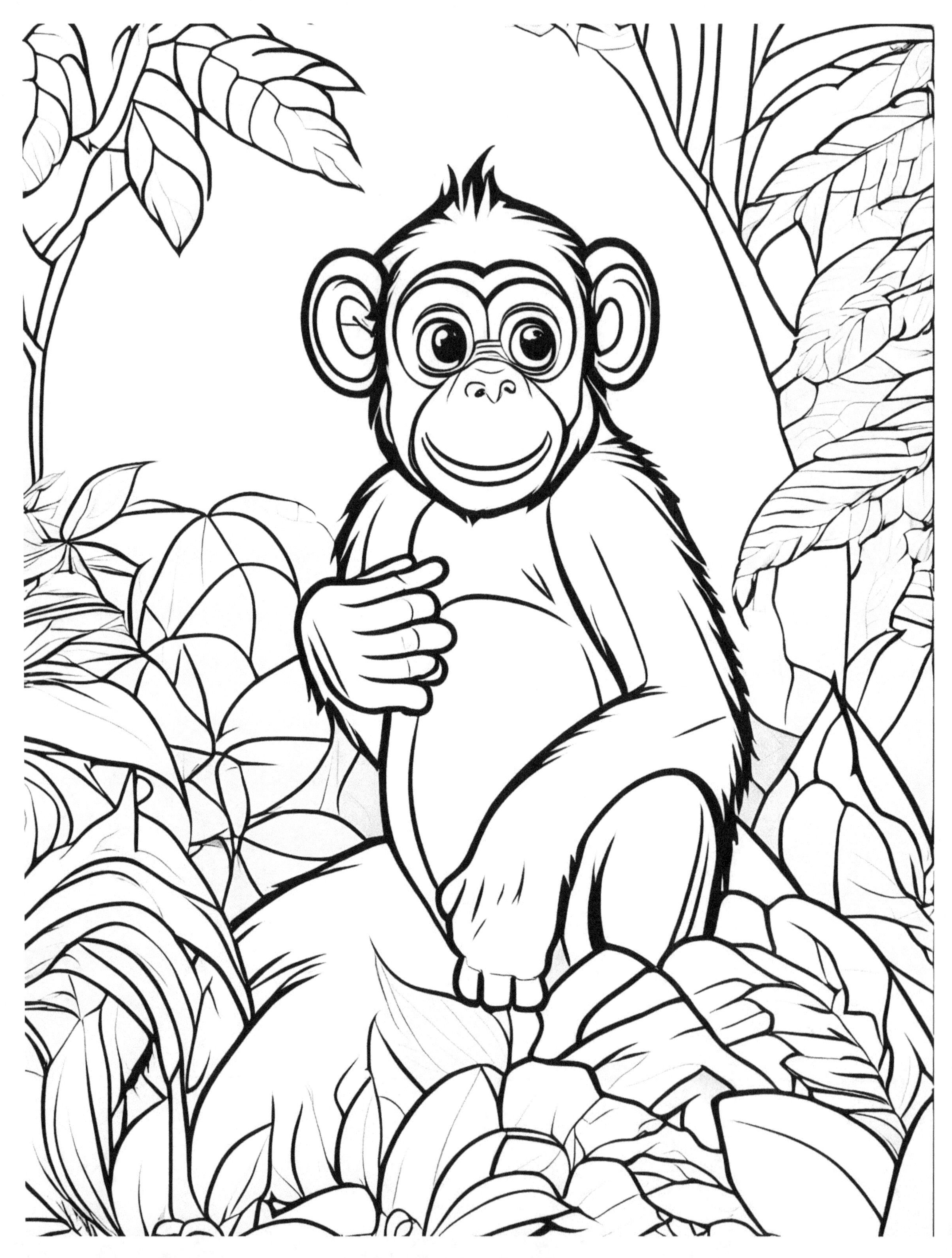

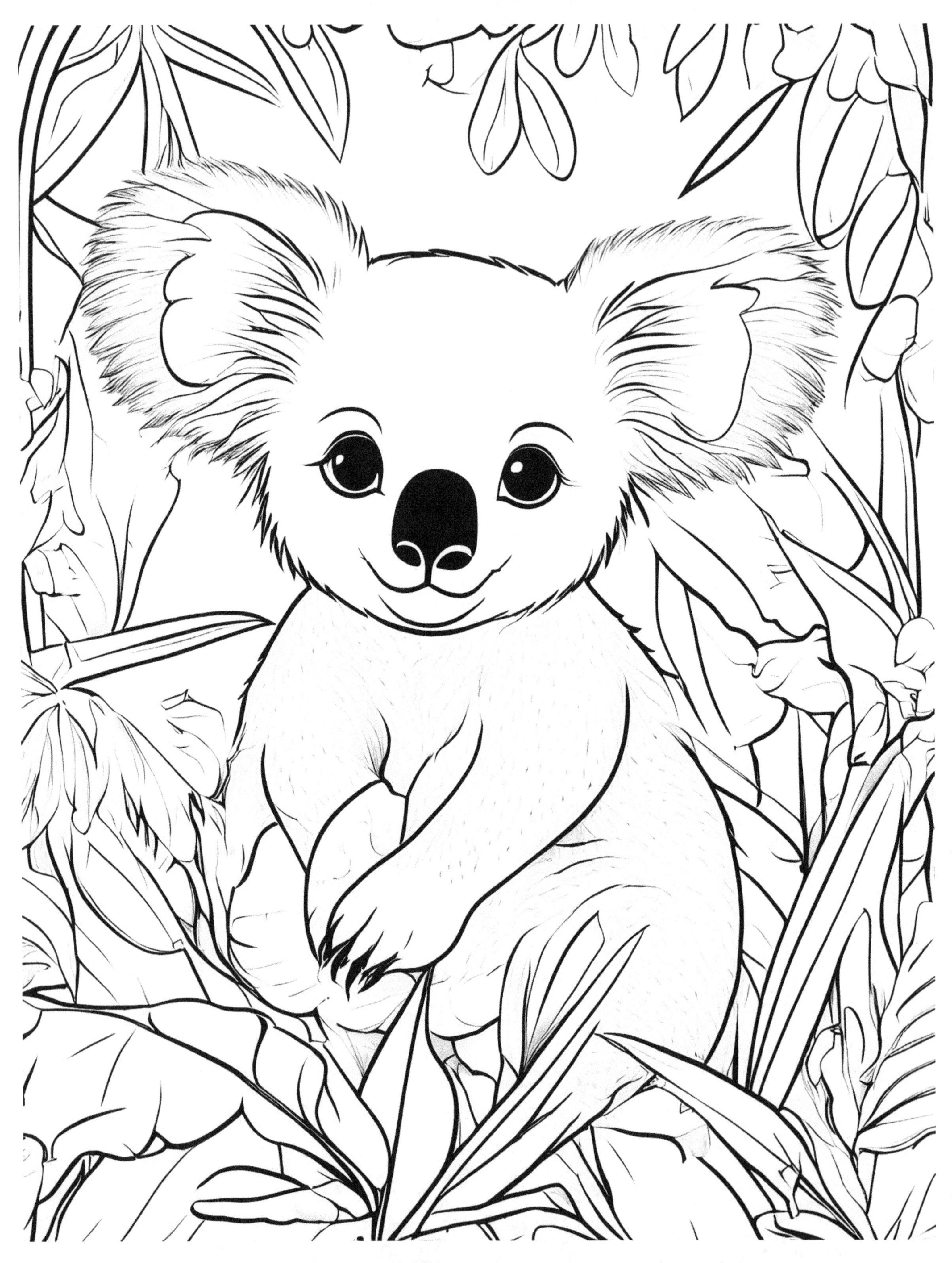

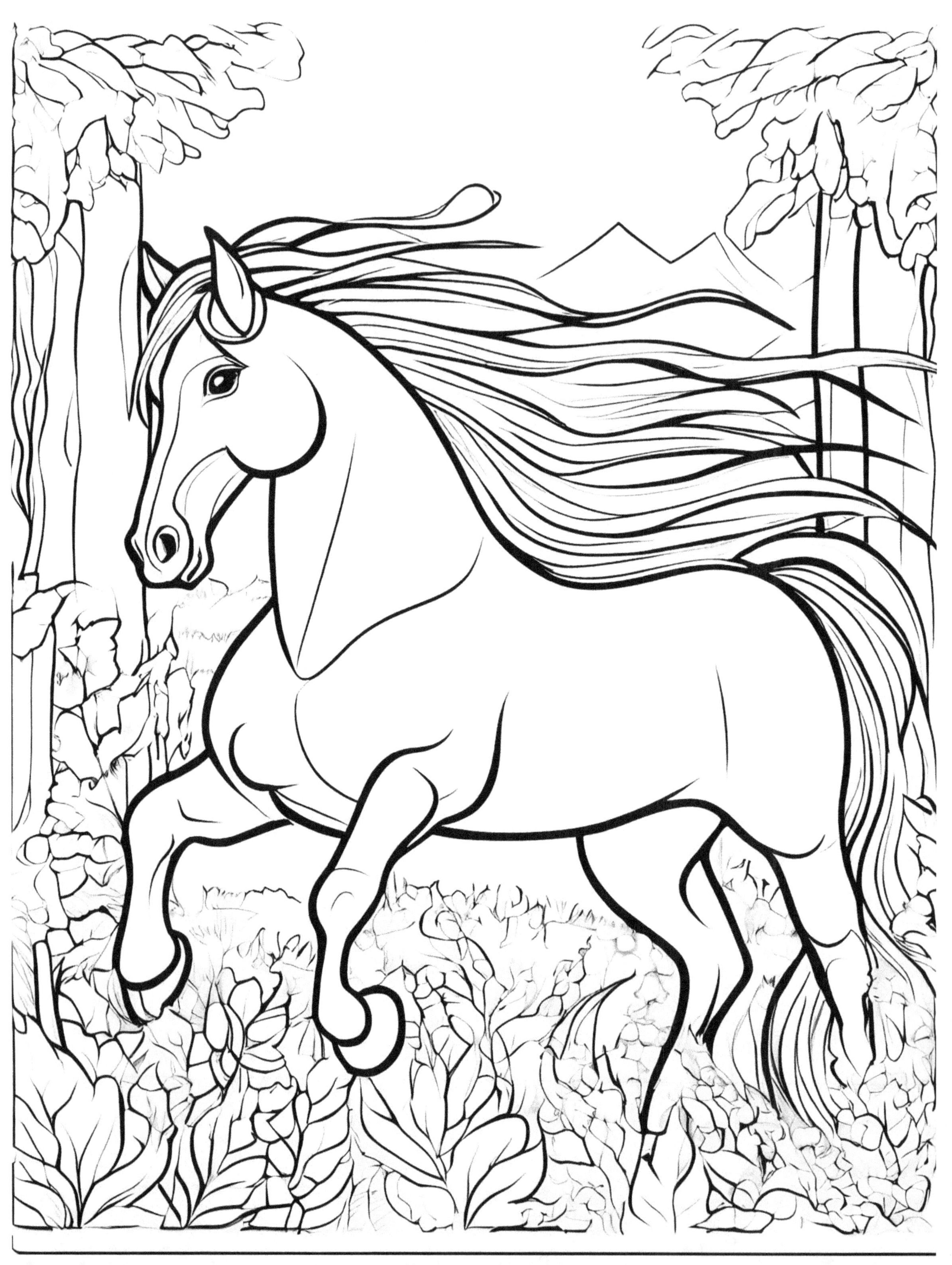

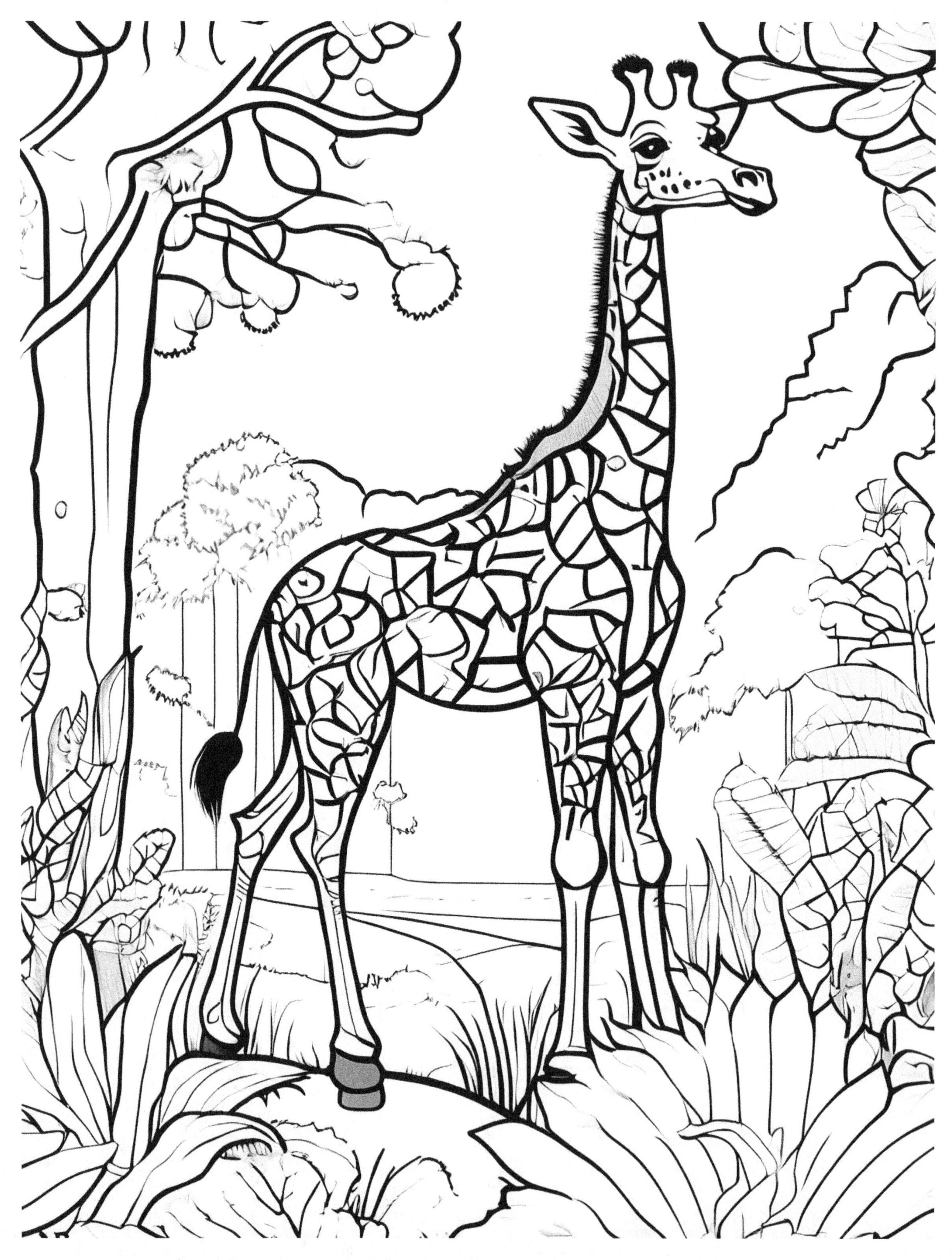

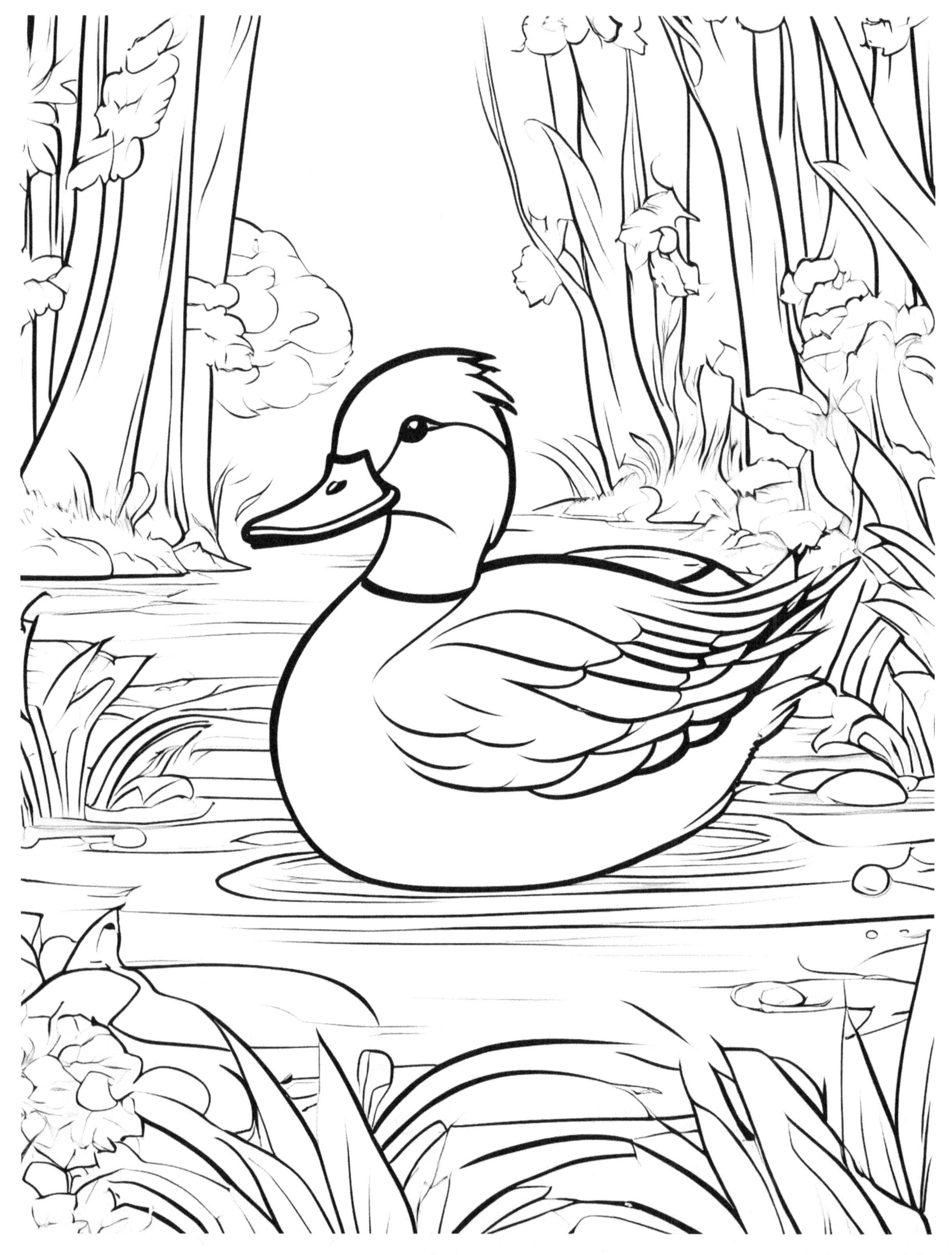

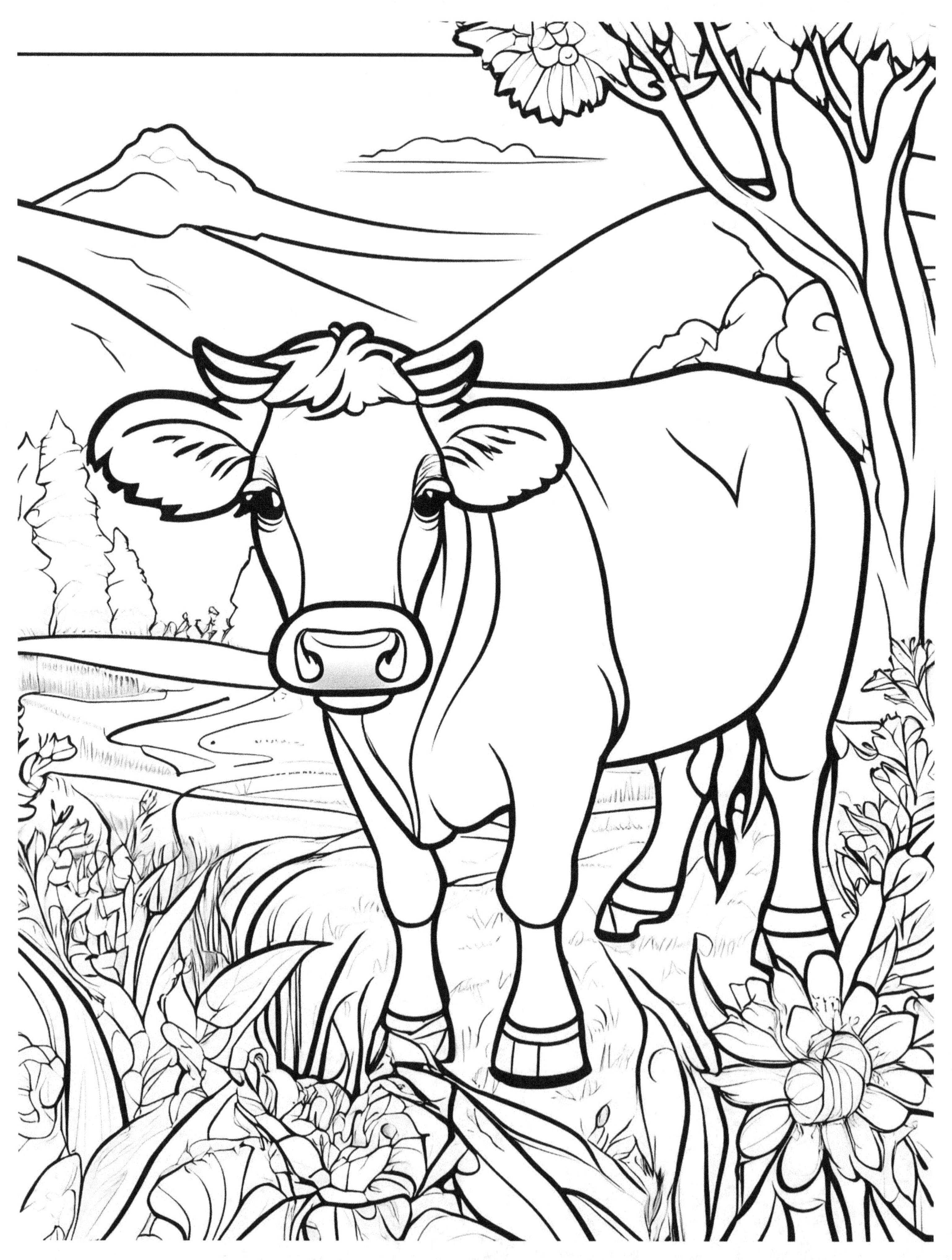

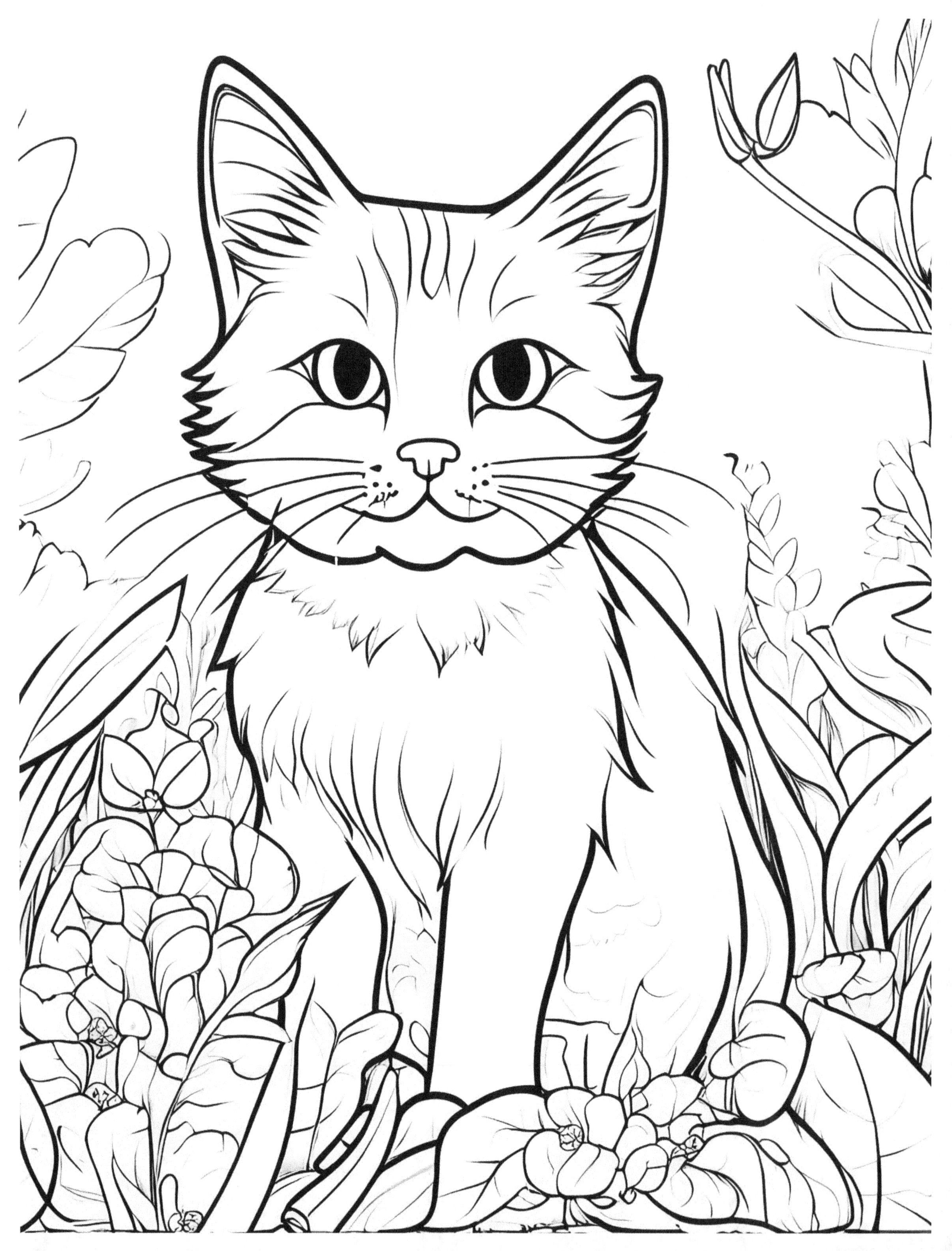

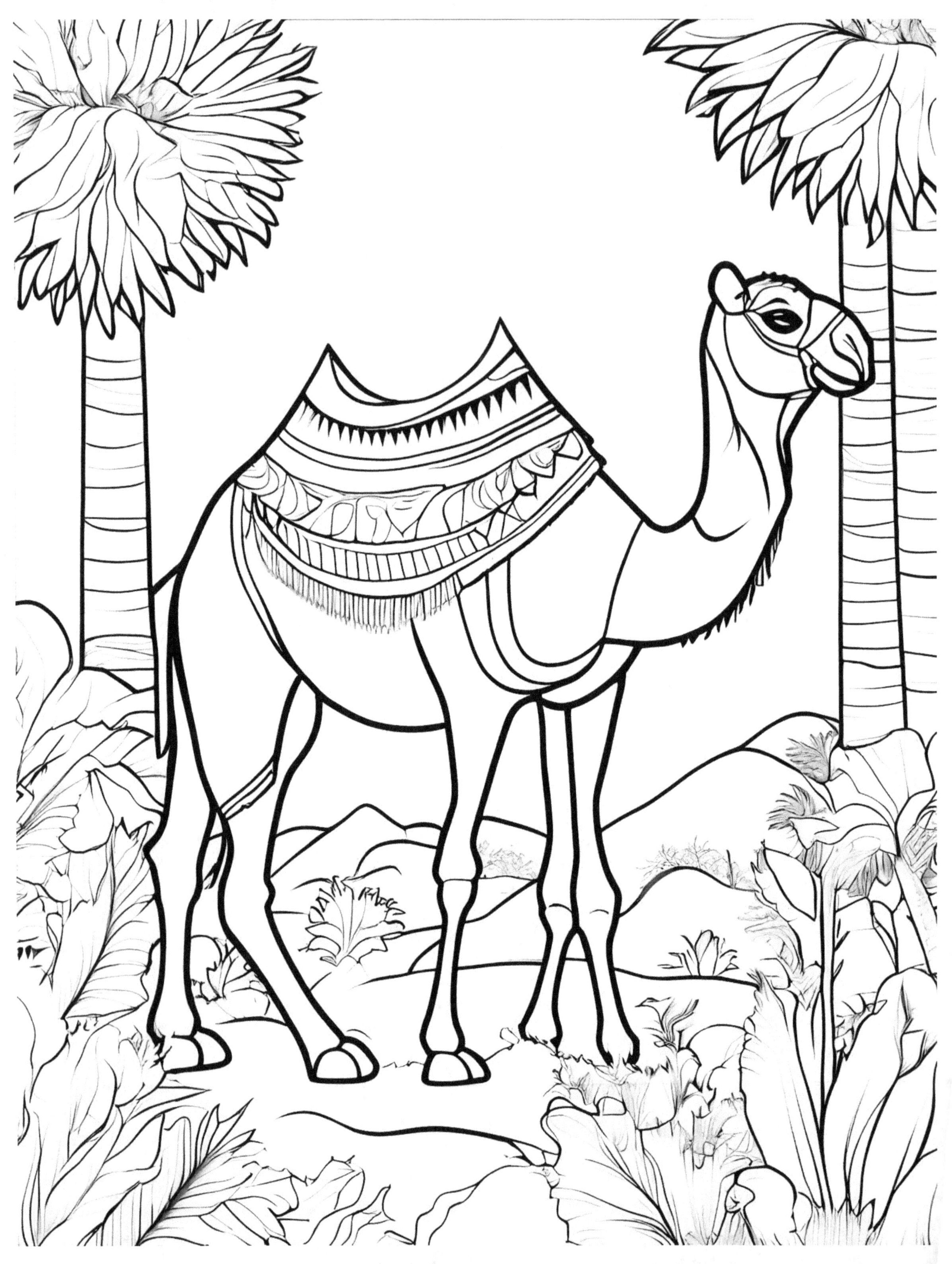